בס"ד תשפ"ג

Dedicated to the memory of our parents

# Larry and Bernice
# Wecker z"l

who deeply valued Jewish education.

# Society and Self

# Society and Self

## On the Writings of
## Rabbi Joseph B. Soloveitchik

### Gerald J. (Ya'akov) Blidstein

OU**PRESS**

New York

Library of Congress Cataloging-in-Publication Data

ISBN 978-1-60280-204-9

Manufactured in the United States of America

*Published by*
OU Press
an imprint of the Orthodox Union
11 Broadway
New York, NY 10004
www.oupress.org
oupress@ou.org

*Distributed by*
KTAV Publishing House, Inc.
888 Newark Avenue
Jersey City, NJ 07306
Tel. (201) 963-9524
Fax. (201) 963-0102
www.ktav.com
bernie@ktav.com

This publication was made possible with the support of
the Katz and Straus Families

*In Commemoration of*

the Birth of Our Grandson

שלמה יששכר
בן בנימין מאיר ושרה אביבה
Samuel Issachar Bick Katz

November 13, 2011      ט"ז חשון תשע"ב

*Dedicated by*
Mordecai D. and Dr. Monique C. Katz

*In Loving Memory of Our Parents*

Joseph and Gwendolyn Straus
יוסף שמואל בן בנימין
גינגדל בת משה יעקב

*Dedicated by*
Moshael and Zahava Straus
Daniel and Joyce Straus

In Memory of My Mother

CELIA BLIDSTEIN ע"ה

A woman of great
loyalty, courage, and wisdom

Slutsk   1908
Beersheba   2010

# Contents

Introduction                                    11

A Religious-Zionist Thinker?                    19

Letters on Public Affairs                       37

Biblical Models                                 63

The Jewish People                               77

"Fate" and "Destiny"                           105

The Covenant of Marriage                       111

The Norms and Nature of Mourning               121

On Death                                       139

Chapter Sources                                153

About the Author                               155

# Introduction

The materials presented in this book reflect, by and large, my thoughts regarding the writings of the Rav, Rabbi Joseph B. Soloveitchik, over the last decades. As I look at these essays, I realize that I engaged mostly in exposition, which is perhaps a natural stance for a former student to adopt. By and large, I address the question: What does the Rav say? Except for some minor editorial adjustments, I have not made changes in what I wrote over the years, although in a small number of instances I added some comments in footnotes. By and large, then, these essays speak out of the past, though I shall argue that at least as regards a number of topics, they also reflect the present.

The present I wish to discuss is that reflected in the current appropriation of the thought of Rabbi Soloveitchik by the religious culture of contemporary Israel. By definition, my thoughts are impressionistic; they do not claim verification by any social science criterion. But I do think they accurately represent the current situation.

In general, Rabbi Soloveitchik has been adopted by the nonharedi mainstream. He is a legitimate religious voice, one which is increasingly heard. A visitor to Friday night services in an Israeli synagogue has a good chance of encountering a quotation from the work of the Rav in the *d'var Torah* given by the synagogue rabbi or a member of the congregation, irrespective of their ethnic identity. Basic categories introduced by the Rav (say *brit goral* and *brit ye'ud;* the very phrase *ish halakhah);* are almost *lingua franca.* The Rav's Hebrew writings, especially "Kol Dodi Dofek" and the translation of "Lonely Man of Faith," have long been part of the religious school curriculum, and this has had no small impact in establishing his legitimacy and relevance.

The Rav's religious depth is acknowledged. This is perhaps not as trivial an achievement as it may seem. For the cultural scene is still very much dominated by the school of R. Kook. Most people citing the Rav, including adherents of R. Kook, are aware that he represents a different perspective on a number of issues, that he pursues a different agenda. Nonetheless, the Rav has become an attractive figure. His profundity is appreciated by the religious seeker, and his noninsularity is admired (if at a distance). The Rav himself represents the possibility, indeed the propriety, of achieving true Torah eminence while also remaining open to the positive aspects of modernity. Here and there, students of the Rav, identified as such, do become admired role models.

There are, however, some topics about which the Rav has not succeeded in communicating his vision. There is, first, his moderate, realistic, view of Zionism and the State of Israel, although it is possible that the messianic view of the State and of the processes involved in its establishment and continued existence is being reconsidered. In this regard the Rav himself may be a formative influence, but this is happening at a very deep—and as yet unarticulated—level. In one of the essays of this volume, I argued that the Rav is not a Zionist thinker. This may have been a hasty, superficial, judgment. But I would still assert that Israel and the Zionist enterprise are not at the center of the Rav's thought. The Rav's discussion of Purim in *Days of Deliverance* is perhaps typical: most religionists here focus on the Jews of Persia as exemplifying the destiny of a stateless community, as almost deserving their diaspora fate. But the Rav read the problem of vulnerability, even (indeed especially!) on an individual basis, as the heart of the story. This is not a trivial difference. Indeed, vulnerability is a basic component of the human personality and the person's existence for the Rav and, perhaps for most thinking people today. Of course, the fact that the Rav has a human agenda (as opposed to a strictly ideological one) is one of the factors that brings him an audience; his readers recognize themselves—their fears and qualms—in these writings.

When the Rav died, the question asked most frequently (at least of myself) was: Why didn't he live in Israel? Recently I was asked that question again, and I referred the questioner to my essay, which showed that Israel was not at the center of the Rav's spiritual reality. The questioner responded: But that is precisely the problem. I, personally, have no desire to question the Rav's priorities; but my questioner made his point. Nonetheless, I think most are willing to remain puzzled by the Rav's behavior but to suspend judgment and focus on what the Rav can give them in their present situation. Even those who remain critical do not see this issue as contaminating or even undermining the Rav's body of thought. The Rav's "problematic" perspective on Israel has not brought the religious public to reject his stance on other topics or the authority of his person. On a broader level, the religious public has grown accustomed to finding its authority figures outside the boundaries of the State: the Lubavitcher Rebbe and even, in a sense, Braslav. The fact that Israel has not produced a figure of recognized spiritual eminence is an acknowledged problem, pointed out already by the Rav himself in the fifties and sixties.

But there is a more problematic issue, at least (I would imagine) from the Rav's point of view. When the Rav died, I was approached to speak about him by various communities. I assumed that I would "say over" or even expand upon, halakhic discourses of the Rav. *Lo dubim ve-lo ya'ar!* There was no interest in that at all. People were interested— very interested—in hearing the Rav on *teshuva,* or what the Rav said as a *darshan,* and certainly his opinion on issues of the day.

I think this is a problem that goes further than the Rav, at least in Israel. It is not merely a matter of the long-standing difficulty in persuading people of the broad vitality of halakhic discourse, or of the value of making the effort necessary to master the intensity of its intricate texts, a problem going back to Talmudic times, when popular interest in aggadah outstripped that in halakhah. Furthermore, the Rav claims that ideologically, only the substance of a halakhic reality testifies to the authenticity of this or that element in Jewish thought. This too has not been accepted, as halakhah is hardly the litmus test for Jewish authenticity. To put the matter symbolically, *Ish ha-Halakhah* is the least read of the major works, and its protagonists are not the heroes of Jewish spirituality. Its anecdotes and narrative incidents have survived and are frequently cited—but the matter does not go further than that. The community acknowledges the authority of halakhah but not its intellectual, cognitive, value. By and large, the community accepts the fact that change must accommodate halakhah, must meet the halakhic standard. But it is not fascinated by study of halakhah—neither that of the yeshiva nor that of academe. An Israeli *rosh yeshiva* (not of Alon Shevut!) once told me how much he envies his American counterparts (by which he meant students of the Rav) whose students retain their interest in learning after leaving yeshiva. There is an obvious naiveté here, but the basic judgment is interesting. Put perhaps more generously, the community does not adopt the Rav's view of what halakhah is. Other topics seem to attract. Studying with the Rav was an experience of high adventure. I do not think that the study of halakhah has retained that character for most religious Israelis. It is not at the center of their Jewish reality, certainly not at its peak.

In making this observation I hardly mean to deny the Rav's central role in putting halakhah on the agenda of the Jewish community. It is certainly the case that the normative aspect of Judaism is acknowledged—and positively so—as an undeniable characteristic of Jewish existence. This marks a sea-change compared to the atmosphere in the nineteenth and early twentieth century. But I still feel that for many today, halakhah is neither the intellectual or spiritual axis that the Rav thought it should be.

* * *

Looking at the photographs of the Rav surrounded in *shiur* by his students, I can't help noticing how young we all were. I wonder how much this explains! Of course, the Rav spoke to all ages (as the hundreds who crowded Lamport auditorium to hear the *yahrzeit shiur* or those who came to hear him Saturday nights in Boston testified), and his writings continue to do so. The Talmud *shiur*, though, was exclusively halakhic. It had no philosophic content or even overtones. This fact has surprised many who never participated in the *shiur* and have assumed that what fascinated the Rav were Barth and Scheler, but not Ba'al HaMa'or and Rabbenu Tam. Perhaps, too, the Rav knew that the younger student could master halakhic intricacies and sources, but that a deep appreciation of religious philosophy and existential anguish needed more seasoning and experience.

Be this as it may, the Rav demonstrated, weekly, that halakhah was an engrossing commitment; if he brought something of value to his young audience—aside from the analyses themselves—it was just that. Needless to say, the Rav did not present his *shiur* as a polemic or as an educational platform. You were either engaged by the analysis or not; and if not, there was nothing for you to do but to sit it out. But even the student who sat it out knew full well (I believe) that he was witness to a moment of high import.

What explains the excitement, the electricity in the air? There is of course no formula for intellectual charisma. Nonetheless, I will advance a number of suggestions. First, it will not do to speak of charisma (even detailing the techniques by which charisma is produced) without acknowledging the constant presence of reverence, even of awe. Most students trembled, I think, not only for fear that their ignorance or lack of proper preparation would be exposed. It was likely, moreover, that the Rav tapped into the ever-present problem of religious identity and modernity. There were many ways in which he served as exemplar in a world that offered few models but much anguish. This was especially the situation insofar as the figures teaching Torah were concerned. We knew the Rav was different, and we were pleased by that. The body language—in the broadest sense of the term—was modern, that is to say normal. Paradoxically, it was this normality that so won his students over. We probably didn't realize how much he shared with the world we did not inhabit.

Moreover, the Rav presumed to handle and recast the holiest of data, the very tradition itself. He was not repeating what the text said, by any means. He was presenting, from the first moment on, a new perception of what the Talmud or the *rishonim* meant. This new perception provided insight, a plunge into the depths of how the Talmudic categories could be defined, how they could operate. You could take it or leave it, but you really couldn't remain intellectually apathetic. This new perception introduced a set of coordinates that were not at all identical with those explicitly set out by the Talmud and required a reorientation. The new perception created a new halakhic cosmos, as tree after tree becomes an organic part of the new forest. Being present at creation is obviously exciting. Often, a measure of problem solving was involved. (I think it was far easier to learn from the Rav how to identify the problem than how to devise the solution; the latter required true creativity!) The Rav speaks much (in *Halakhic Man*) of creativity and novelty, and his own halakhic work was a systematic expression of this demand, a rejection of study that did not achieve (or aim at) creativity. So that aware as we were of the creativity that characterized what the Rav did, I don't think we thought of it in terms of novelty, as though we witnessed a revolution; what we heard was, we were convinced, what the Talmud was saying—an interesting combination of traditionalist creativity. Familiar as we all were with the spoon-feeding and repetition characterizing most university lectures, we found in the Rav a constant stimulus, an uncompromising commitment to intellectual rigor. The assignments were stiff, and the *shiur* was not a place one went to relax. You were expected (by yourself, at least) to walk in having given the materials some thought. I also knew some few students who reacted negatively to the Rav's recasting of halakhic texts. They were not incapable of making the necessary recalibration but rather marched to a different tune. Planting the new trees often required their uprooting from ancestral soil. But in truth, the overwhelming majority were swept along enthusiastically, thoroughly accepting their radically new experience and thoroughly identifying with the master teacher who made it all possible.

This creative, innovative, thrust did not lead the Rav in the direction of critical Talmud study. I have reason to believe he thought that such study led to trivial results. The basic issues, those he found worth exploring, emerged from study of the Talmudic text and context as we have them and from study of those *rishonim* who were studied in the classical milieu. This was not only an ideological position; it also reflected his own experience, which found no need for an alternative method and was not troubled by an alternative problematic. I doubt, in other words, that his rejection of critical method derived—at least consciously—from apprehension as to its possibly anti-nomian implications. The issue, as he saw it, was much more intellectual and methodological, though by that I do not mean to say that he would have been comfortable with the nontraditionalism that informs much critical method (though it has been shown that *rishonim* incorporate critical moves in their work). Historicism was in the air, and he felt a need to respond to it in some of his published work—a not-so-critical method, which had few if any adherents in the audience he addressed. That has remained the case, as the adherents of philological method (asking of any text how it was originally formulated, what it meant at its origin and in its original context) hardly rival in numbers those of the more currently traditional approaches. The Rav never felt the need to respond to the style of doing Talmud found in universities.

It is clear, even from this last comment, that the Rav was methodologically self-conscious. In a sense, *Halakhic Man* is an essay in method, as is the eulogy for R. Velvel. This does not necessarily mark the Rav as a modernist; the great medieval scholars were also self-aware, conscious of what they were—and were not—doing. But I recall the Rav making a comment that disclosed how profoundly self-conscious he was: "Were I to meet R. Akiva on the street, I would not know what to say to him, but I would have no trouble conversing with Abaye if I met him on the street." Was this a confession of disconnection, or a comment on the significance of method? I do not know how many of my contemporaries realized how unsettling (and empowering) this comment could be; nor do I know how many of the Rav's peers could make such a comment to their students or to themselves. Be this as it may, this insight did not prevent the Rav from continuing the *shiur*.

\* \* \*

I am very pleased that this collection of my essays devoted to the writings of the Rav has been published in the OU Press series of publications. I would like to thank Rabbi Menachem Genack, General Editor of the OU Press, for incorporating my work in the series and authorizing the translations from the Hebrew original. Naturally, my thanks to the translators for their work, and to Rabbi Simon Posner, Executive Editor of the OU Press, for his efforts in bringing this volume to press. Above all, I would like to express my appreciation to Dr. Joel B. Wolowelsky, who approached me with the suggestion for the book, and did much of the original editorial work needed to make it a reality. I acknowledge as well the generous assistance for this publication provided by Mordecai and Dr. Monique Katz, Moshael and Zahava Straus, and Daniel and Joyce Straus.

# A Religious-Zionist Thinker?

## I

Rabbi Joseph B. Soloveitchik is commonly counted among the philosophers of Religious-Zionism. In any event, so one would understand from several articles devoted to the issue. Walter Wurzburger writes about "the philosophical foundations of Rabbi Soloveitchik's Religious-Zionist thought,"[1] and so too is it implied in Michael Rosenak's discussion of the Rav's teachings, "'The Jewish Person' and the State."[2] Dov Schwartz examines "Rabbi Soloveitchik's Teachings in Light of Religious-Zionist Thought: Secularization and the State,"[3] and he also relates to central themes in the Rav's teachings as part of the very essence of this thought in his book, "Faith at a Crossroad."[4] Aviezer Ravitzky is careful not to assert that the Rav himself developed a Religious-Zionist creed, but he is ready to describe a "Religious-Zionist position," that is maintained, among others, by "students of Rabbi Joseph B. Soloveitchik in Israel and abroad."[5]

Without a doubt the Rav publicly identified with Religious-Zionism and contributed to it of his prestige, authority, and standing. For years he served as "honorary president" of the Mizrachi movement in

---

[1] Walter S. Wurtzburger, "*Ha-Yesodot ha-Filosofiyim be-Mishnato ha-Tziyonit Datit shel ha-Rav Soloveitchik*," in Avi Sagi (ed.), *Emunah bi-Zemanim Mishtanim: Al Mishnato shel ha-Rav Yosef Dov Soloveitchik*, Jerusalem: Sifriyat Elinor, 5757, pp. 111–22.

[2] Michael Rosenak, "'*Ha-Adam ha-Yehudi' ve-ha-Medinah*," in Shaul Israeli, Nachum Lamm, and Yitzchak Refael (eds.), *Sefer Yovel li-Khevod Morenu ha-Gaon Yosef Dov ha-Levi Soloveitchik*, I, Jerusalem: Mossad Ha-Rav Kook, 5744, pp. 152–69.

[3] Dov Schwartz, "*Mishnato shel ha-Rav Soloveitchik bi-Re'i he-Hagut ha-Tziyonit Datit: Ha-Hilun ve-ha-Medinah*," in Sagi (ed.), *Emunah bi-Zemanim Mishtanim*, pp. 123–48.

[4] Dov Schwartz, *Emunah al Parashat Derakhim*, Tel-Aviv: Am Oved, 5756, pp. 54–60, 235–54.

[5] Aviezer Ravitzky, "*Ha-Tzafui ve-ha-Reshut Netunah*," in Aluf Har-Even (ed.), *Yisrael Likrat ha-Me'ah ha-21: Hazon ve-Ya'adim*, Jerusalem: Van Leer Institute, 5744, p. 185. See also his words in note 10.

the United States, spoke at its annual conventions, and was even involved in its activities. He asked his students to join the ranks of Mizrachi, and in broader fashion he called for action that would benefit the State of Israel. While he sharply criticized the secular leadership of the state and its violation of the holiness of Israel, he came out no less forcefully against the Haredi world that estranged itself from the state. Let it be immediately said: the Haredi world did not forgive anything of the Rav's positions and personality, including his Zionist activity. There is no question then that the Rav was a Religious-Zionist, though he was less than fond of this strange label.[6]

## II

In light of these positions and statements, is there room to question Rabbi Soloveitchik's classification as a Religious-Zionist thinker? Is it not clear beyond all doubt that he supported the Zionist enterprise and at the same time uncompromisingly insisted on the importance of the religious character of the newly-founded state? While it is true that the Rav's Zionism did not include a messianic component, this certainly does not preclude his placement in the Religious-Zionist camp. Surely there is no doubt that the Rav saw the rebirth of the State of Israel as an act of heavenly Providence, "an almost supernatural occurrence," "redemption."[7] Even his lack of excitement regarding the designation "Religious-Zionism" and his statement that were he forced to choose between the God of Israel and the State of Israel, he would opt for the former, do not cast doubts about his fundamental orientation or even hint at any misgivings about Religious-Zionism. Indeed, the Rav never concealed, to put it mildly, this sympathy, for which, according to him, he paid a significant personal price: "I was not born into a Zionist house . . . I now identify

---

[6] Joseph B. Soloveitchik, *Five Addresses*, trans. S. M. Lehrman and A. H. Rabinowitz (Jerusalem: Tal Orot Institute, 5743), p. 36. This is a translation of the Rav's *Hamesh Derashot* (Jerusalem: Tal Orot Institute, 5734).

[7] Ibid. p. 32; Joseph B. Soloveitchik, *Fate and Destiny: From the Holocaust to the State of Israel* (Hoboken, 2000), p. 26. This is a translation of "Kol Dodi Dofek." The Hebrew version has been reprinted many times, most recently in *Emunah BeZman Mashber*, part of Yediot's Am HaSefer series. References in this volume are to the English translation by Lawrence Laplan, published as *Faith and Destiny: From the Holocaust to the State of Israel* (KTAV, 2002).

with Mizrachi . . . I built an altar . . . the altar still stands today, with smoke rising from the sacrifice upon it."[8]

Even if there is no place for doubts about Rabbi Soloveitchik's being a Religious-Zionist leader, it seems to me that there is room to ask whether he should be viewed as a Religious-Zionist thinker. There is no questioning the Rav's organizational affiliation or his constant and faithful public activity for the benefit of Religious-Zionism. So too there is no doubt that his general thought has Zionist ramifications, in those places where the general principles that guided him accord with and enrich his Religious-Zionist teachings. But there is still room to ask whether these facts suffice to justify discussing the Rav in the framework of Religious-Zionist thought, whether he should be located in the ranks of this school, and whether his Religious-Zionist principles should be seen as principles that enriched his thinking in general.

The first reason for my questioning the identification of Rabbi Soloveitchik as a Religious-Zionist thinker is very simple. Anyone who examines the Rav's writings will see that discussion of the Zionist or Religious-Zionist problem constitutes only a very small portion of his work. The great majority of his articles deal with other issues: the nature of the spiritual experience, the nature of the halakhic experience, the standing of the individual vis-à-vis the community, and the like. These issues, in addition to purely halakhic topics, are the cornerstones of the Rav's intellectual, spiritual, and conceptual world. Anyone who

---

[8] *Five Addresses*, pp. 34–36. It is true that the Rav sacrificed "sleepless nights" on that altar, but in light of the context, it would seem that the primary cause was his detachment from family tradition. Without a doubt his description of the detachment of the early leaders of Religious-Zionism from their natural circles and their isolation matches the Rav's experience: "Loneliness is the loss of contact between man and the world in which he grew up, and in which he spent his childhood . . . he who joined the Mizrachi was virtually excluded from his birthplace and ostracised from his spiritual paternal home . . . from the leaders of the generation . . . from the saintly ones of the generation . . . and the yawning gap that had grown between him and his brothers caused him much sorrow. To be separated from his outstanding brothers . . . was a tragedy for Joseph" (pp. 25–26). The Rav adds that he was overcome on those nights by "doubts and reservations." It seems that the non-Zionist tradition of "my parents' ancestors" continued to attract him, and that he became convinced "of the correctness of our movement's path" only after the Holocaust and the establishment of the State of Israel (p. 36).

reads his major treatises—*Halakhic Man,*[9] *The Lonely Man of Faith,*[10] *U-Vikashtem mi-Sham,*[11] and *Mah Dodekh mi-Dod*[12]—and his regular lectures on prayer and repentance will immediately understand what I mean. Religious-Zionism did not preoccupy the Rav on the theoretical-conceptual level, it did not set his spiritual or intellectual agenda, and Religious-Zionist thinkers are not his intellectual peers. Furthermore, anyone who considers the theoreticians of Religious-Zionism will see before him a list of thinkers whose Zionism filled their consciousness and dominated their thinking, people who dedicated the greater part of their intellectual energy to the issue. Not so the Rav.

On the face of it, my argument is undermined by the essay, "Kol Dodi Dofek" ("Hark, My Beloved Knocks"), the title of which already alludes to the establishment of the State of Israel and which deals extensively with this issue. One essay, however, does not compensate for what is lacking, nor testify to constant and lasting preoccupation with the topic. Moreover, anyone who reads "Kol Dodi" will see that its conceptual component is not dedicated to the question of Zionism and statehood or to the problems arising from the combination of the two. The primary conceptual discussion relates to a description of the "covenant of fate" and the "covenant of destiny" and to the importance of these concepts for understanding Jewish history across the generations, and especially the Holocaust and modernity. What we have here is national and religious thinking that deals with the nature of the existence of the nation in the present and with the relationship of the members of the people one to the other. The concepts of "covenant of fate" and "covenant of destiny" characterize also and perhaps especially what is happening in Zion, and anyone who so desires can hear echoes of the Zion-

---

[9] Joseph B. Soloveitchik, *Halakhic Man,* trans. Lawrence Kaplan (Philadelphia, PA: Jewish Publication Society, 1983). Originally published in Hebrew under the title *Ish ha-Halakhah, Talpiot* I, nos. 3–4 (1944); republished in Pinhas Peli, ed., *Be-Sod ha-Yahid ve-ha-Yahad* (Jerusalem: Orot, 5736 [1976]), pp. 37–188.

[10] Joseph B. Soloveitchik, "The Lonely Man of Faith," *Tradition* 7, 2 (Summer, 1965), pp. 5–68. Available at www.traditiononline.org.

[11] Joseph B. Soloveitchik, *U-Vikashtem mi-Sham, Hadarom no. 47, Tishrei 5739* (1979). Recently issued as *And From There You Shall Seek,* trans. Naomi Goldblum (KTAV, 2008).

[12] Joseph B. Soloveitchik, "*Mah Dodekh mi-Dod,*" in *Be-Sod ha-Yahid ve-ha-Yahad,* pp. 189–254.

ist reality in this discussion. But they are not unique to this reality, and their discussion does not deal with it in explicit or prominent manner.[13] It seems that even one who argues that the creation of the concepts "covenant of fate" and "covenant of destiny" was directed primarily at the Zionist reality, to the problematic attitude toward religiously non-observant Jews in the context of the return to Zion and establishment of a state, must agree that the exclusive discussion of this issue leaves many other fundamental issues untreated. This conceptual discourse includes the Zionist-political issue, but is not totally devoted to it.[14]

The essay, "Kol Dodi Dofek," translated as *Fate and Destiny*, deals at length with the State of Israel, but its essential tenor is sermonizing, and not conceptual. It comes to answer the question how American Jews, and primarily observant Jews, should relate to the state in actual practice. The background is clearly historical (the destruction of European Jewry is strongly present throughout the essay) rather than conceptual. The Rav describes the echoes of Providence that could be heard in the course of the establishment of the state. He demands loyalty to the State of Israel, in light of Heaven's intercession on its behalf. But there is no conceptual struggle with the full gamut of practical and

---

[13] In this volume's chapter "The Jewish People," I noted the verbal and conceptual parallel between the concepts of "fate" and "destiny" and those of "Schiksal" and "Bestimmungsgefühl" in the writings of Martin Buber. This pair of concepts was used in Germany during the period that the Rav was there (so too the term "Schicksalgemeinschaft"), though these concepts were developed in the Rav's writings in a way that accorded with his own ideas and time. In contrast, Ehud Luz comments that "the idea [if not the terms] are already found in the early writings of the Religious-Zionist thinkers," and he cites as an example the writings of R. Mordekhai Eliasberg and the Netziv in the nineteenth century and of R. Kook in the twentieth century. See Ehud Luz, "*Gevulot ha-Sovlanut*," in Shmuel Almog, Yehuda Reinhartz and Anita Shapira (eds.), *Tziyonut Datit*, Jerusalem: Merkaz Zalman Shazar, 5754, pp. 56–58. Regarding Rabbi Reines, see Dov Schwartz, *Etgar u-Mashber be-Hug ha-Rav Kook*, Tel-Aviv: Am Oved, 5761, pp. 224–26. In any case, the deep structure of the existence of a "covenant of fate" alongside a "covenant of destiny" also suits the halakhic reality regarding the status of Jews who identify as Jews, even though they are nonobservant.

[14] The characterization mentioned above applies also to the question of the relationship between Religious-Zionism to other issues in the Rav's thought. Thus, Michael Rosenak demonstrates how the Zionist idea accords with central issues in the Rav's thought ("'*Ha-Adam ha-Yehudi*' *ve-ha-Medinah*"). However, the Rav hardly mentions Zionism at all in those discussions. As Ravitzky summarizes: "In Rabbi Soloveitchik's essays and *derashot*, conceptual foundations are developed, upon which one could establish basic principles such as these. It is doubtful that the Rav himself fully reached these conclusions. In any event, they were not drawn in an unequivalent manner in his words or in his life" ("*Ha-Tzafui ve-ha-Reshut Netunah*," p. 191).

conceptual phenomena that Zionism entails, nor even a historiosophic struggle with the place of Zionism in Judaism's world view. Indeed, the public framework in which the lecture was delivered—a synagogue sermon on the occasion of the celebration of Israel Independence Day—was inappropriate for a discussion of this kind.[15]

The quantitative balance slightly tips the moment we consider the Rav's homiletical oeuvre. Here the Religious-Zionist issue frequently arises, and we even find an entire volume—*Five Addresses*—devoted to the issue. It seems to me, however, that this homiletical occupation does not stand up against the Rav's primary philosophical occupation. This assessment does not relate to the importance of the works but to the circumstances in which they came into being and their classification. The homilies, in effect, constitute community work, a response to the needs of the Religious-Zionist community, and even an expression of the Rav's leadership of this community, but not independent philosophical contemplation. When the Rav comes to set his intellectual agenda, he does not turn to the issues that he expounded before the Religious-Zionist public. The same is true regarding the Rav's intellectual peer group. Anyone who examines the Rav's philosophical articles will not find references to the ideas of Religious-Zionist thinkers, but rather explicit struggle with contemporary European thought. Religious-Zionist thought does not appear to have left an impression upon him. I allow myself to surmise that he would not be upset were he denied the title of "Religious-Zionist thinker."

Without a doubt Rabbi Soloveitchik's thought is likely to support a Zionist position, and Michael Rosenak presented such a position.[16] What is more, components of his thought parallel certain themes in Religious-Zionist thought, such as the positive attitude toward human initiative in history. It seems, however, that the matrix of the Rav's position was not the Zionist enterprise and the discussion surrounding it in various religious circles, but rather the place of technological man as "the creator of worlds" in the modern Western world in general, and the desire to argue the Jewish authenticity of such activity. It

---

[15] At the end of this chapter we shall discuss another aspect of this essay.

[16] See Rosenak, "*Ha-Adam ha-Yehudi ve-ha-Medinah.*"

seems to me that the issues raised by modernity and the relationship (or contrast) between that world and the world of the believing and Torah-observant Jew preoccupied the Rav conceptually more than did the Zionist enterprise.

The Rav also did not feel compelled to analytically explain the legitimacy of Zionism or conceptually justify his support of the Zionist movement. I have not found that he dealt with the ideological argument brought against Zionism by its religious opponents: bringing the Messiah, redeeming Israel, changing the historical fate of the nation—these are tasks falling upon God, rather than man. In traditional terms, Zionism "forces the end"; and in less archaic terms, it denies God's exclusive Providence in the world. It seems that the Rav was not impressed by this argument. Perhaps he knew that his great-grandfather, Rabbi Yosef Dov Halevi Soloveitchik, was ready to found a Haredi *Hovevei Zion* movement, but refrained from doing so when he understood that the leadership of the Yishuv was unmistakably secular. Thus we see that the issue was not the ideological concern about "forcing the end" or denial of God's governance of history but the actual character of the Zionist movement in its early stages.[17] Indeed, when he came to explain the opposition to Zionism on the part of his uncle, Rabbi Yitzchak Ze'ev Soloveitchik, the Rav rejected the ideological explanation put forward in the Haredi world and adopted a "Brisker" explanation: the state, argues the Rav, "did not find a place in his halakhic thought system or on his scale of halakhic values . . . He was unable to translate the idea of secular political sovereignty into halakhic terms and values."[18]

In my opinion there are several possible reasons why this Haredi argument did not find an attentive ear in the Rav, even at the level of the need to refute or answer it. First of all, as I have just noted, his approach to man's role in the world imposes activity upon him. First Adam, "majestic man," is commanded to build the world and perfect

---

[17] See Ehud Luz, *Makbilim Nifgashim*, Tel-Aviv: Am Oved, 5745, pp. 74, 154. See, however: Aviezer Ravitzky, *Ha-Ketz ha-Meguleh u-Medinat ha-Yehudim*, Tel-Aviv: Am Oved, 5753, pp. 27–35; Yosef Salmon, "*Dat u-Le'umiyut bi-Tenu'at ha-Tziyonut be-Reshitah*," in Yehuda Reinhartz, Yosef Salmon and Gideon Shimoni (eds.), *Le'umiyut u-Politikah Yehudit: Perspektivot Hadashot*, Jerusalem: Merkaz Zalman Shazar, 5757, pp. 113–40.

[18] "*Ma Dodekh mi-Dod*," p. 241.

it with the powers that God gave him. This mission already negates a picture of the world in which man refrains from activity out of the belief that God alone will act on his behalf. National activity is part of that world of activity about which man in general and a Jew in particular was commanded. This active approach seems ever so much more correct in light of the fact that the Rav did not assign messianic significance to the establishment of the state (beyond the "redemption" that it promised in a particular historical context), as if it were an event leading to the end of days.

In any event, the legitimacy of Zionism reflects history and reality, as they revealed themselves to the Rav during the years of the Holocaust. In one of his sermons, he likens the Religious-Zionist to the Biblical Joseph, who sees, ahead of his brothers, what will happen to his family and prepares a safe haven for them. This Joseph is not only the Religious-Zionist, but also the Jew who integrates himself into modernity and dissociates himself from it at one and the same time, in a world that is so different from that of his origins. The Biblical Joseph symbolizes the Jew who sees the rise of Hitler, the extermination, the despair, and the waves of assimilation passing over the people following the destruction. The Rav understood that Joseph prepared for his brothers not only a physical refuge: "In that very nonobservant Israel the future of Torah and traditional Judaism is far more secure that it is here in the Diaspora." Faced with this reality, the Rav had no doubt that "God decided in accord with Joseph against his brothers." It was not a theological principle that decided the matter but his perception of reality. "But in historical questions, those relating to the destiny of the Eternal People, God himself decides as to whose interpretation shall become the 'law.'"[19]

And from here to a feeling no less deep, and also neither analytical nor intellectual. Coming to explain why religious youth in the United States is not excited by the idea of Aliyah to Israel, the Rav writes: "The relationship of Torah youth to the Land of Israel, which is essentially religious, is reflected in this mirror. These young people are familiar with all the value that halakhah attaches to the Holy Land, but this cognition, like all their other knowledge . . . does

---

[19] *Five Addresses*, pp. 32-33.

not integrate with a dynamic experience containing the yearnings of the generations. For this reason, inner trembling is lacking."[20] Once again, the discussion concerning the Land of Israel and Zionism combines with a broader problem, this time educational and psychological. The failure in inculcating these "yearnings" has ramifications in various realms of Jewish existence in the modern period. What is most important for our purposes: the Rav's words regarding the obligation to go on Aliyah and stand behind the state do not rest on conceptual or analytical foundations. He clarifies that the lack of zeal for Zion does not stem from ignorance in its plain sense. The detachment is not from the sources of knowledge. Torah enlightenment and normative commitment—tools in which the Rav generally places his trust—are irrelevant.

These words, penned by the Rav and not delivered in a public lecture, do not establish the halakhic importance of settling the Land of Israel, and the possibility of actualizing a life of halakhah in it. On the contrary, the Rav notes that even halakhic commitment and education towards halakhic living do not guarantee Zionist commitment. Halakhah does not suffice to satiate the soul.[21] The Rav based the readiness to act on "longings" and "yearnings," terms that appear also in his essay, "*U-Vikashtem mi-Sham*," where he expresses himself in intense religious language. While it would not be right to attach excessive importance to a single passage such as this, the Rav's emotional relationship to the people of Israel's experience over the generations is well-known: "The Jew who believes in *Knesset Israel* is the Jew who lives as part of it wherever it is . . . who binds himself with inseparable bonds . . . to the community of Israel throughout the ages." It is true that he adds: "How so? Through the Torah."[22] But it stands to reason that there were also additional feelings and characteristics through which the connection between the individual Jew and the people of Israel was expressed. Even if the Rav did not attach metaphysical standing to the Land of Israel, beyond that which is

---

[20] "*Al Ahavat ha-Torah u-Ge'ulat Nefesh ha-Dor,*" in *Be-Sod ha-Yahid ve-ha-Yahad*, p. 418.

[21] See the title, "*Ha-Hakarah ha-Intelektualit ve-ha-Havayah ha-Emotziyonalit,*" ibid. p. 409.

[22] Pinchas H. Peli, *On Repentance in the Thought and Oral Discourses of Rabbi Joseph B. Soloveitchik* (Jersey City, NJ: Orit, 1970), p. 137.

necessary for halakhah, this does not mean that his attitude toward it exhausted itself solely in halakhic terms.[23]

Zionism obligates every Jew, inasmuch as he harbors "yearnings of the generations." In other words, a Jew who has an organic, natural, healthy, and normal connection to his people, its fate and destiny, its memories, hardships, and hopes, will want to participate in the building of the land and the establishment of the state, and return to Zion. The voices of the generations denied this are clearly heard; they resonate in his soul. The Rav does not see in the fact that essential elements of the state are secular something to prevent the "yearnings of the generations" from identifying with it. The main thing is the craving for the collective return to the Land of Israel, which includes an independent, political foundation. Someone who doesn't share this craving, who doesn't see it in the many texts that he read from childhood, is not only intellectually deprived. He is closed off from the existential dimension of Jewish identity. Regarding the Land of Israel and the state, as in other matters, the Rav did not seek analytic or even halakhic support in the strict sense of the term; he listened to the generations speaking in his blood.

The relationship to Zionism is built then on two foundations. First, Zionism responds to historical reality, to what is demanded at the moment. In the end, even God gave his assent. Second, Zionism responds to the deep craving in the soul of the people, a craving shared by the Rav as well.

Despite the Rav's declaration that halakhic commitment by itself will not arouse people to Zionism and Aliyah, he bases the standing of the state on its halakhic significance. He asserts that the state, as opposed to the government, is not a secular entity. Why? Because "there is total identity between the Land in its sanctity and the state . . . The sanctity of the Land that is conferred upon the state cannot be cancelled and nobody can defile or profane it." What is this "sanctity"? The Rav adopted Nahmanides' definition of the precept of conquering the Land of Israel, and saw in it a halakhic expression of its sanctity—a

---

[23] Compare: Dov Schwartz, "*Eretz ha-Halakhah – Ha-Rav Yosef Dov Soloveitchik ve-Hugo*," *Eretz ha-Mamashut ve-ha-Dimayon: Ma'amadah shel Eretz Israel be-Hagut ha-Tziyonut ha-Datit*, Tel-Aviv: Am Oved, 5757, p. 188, and also in Appendix 2, ibid. p. 246ff.

clearly halakhic approach, for from the perspective of halakhah, there is no sanctity without commands. The precept of conquering the Land of Israel demands "sovereign conquest," that is to say, the foundation of a state.[24]

The Rav, however, added that just as the sanctity of the Land itself is but "the fruit of the supernal inspiration that rests on the nation when it binds with its Maker," so "I understand the entire greatness, value and importance of the state, all the marvel in its rise and in its continued existence, based exclusively on the uniqueness of the nation and its union with the God of Israel."[25] The sanctity of the Land does not exhaust itself in the precept of conquest and the foundation of a Jewish state, but it remains a function of the observance of the precepts on the part of the people of Israel, both the precepts relating to the land as well as the precepts relating to society. The halakhah itself expresses the covenant between God and the people of Israel and stems from it; it is not a condition in a dry contract but rather the fruit of a stormy and continuing encounter—the nation's "union with the God of Israel." The Torah, with its precepts and laws, is an expression of God's love for Israel. The Rav built the love of a man for his wife on their shared commitment to the covenant in his essay, *The Lonely Man of Faith*. The state's fidelity to halakhah also bears emotional weight. In the absence of such fidelity, the emotional ardor is also extinguished. "As a historical-secular creature who is not driven by the covenantal destiny, the state does not captivate me, nor does it light a burning fire within me."[26] Thus, the "yearnings of the generations" are liable to be tested; emotional commitment is not guaranteed.

The Rav's assumption that the "yearnings of the generations" would draw the youth near to the state even in its present cultural-religious state, somewhat contradicts what we just read that the ardor is conditioned on the religious situation prevailing in the state. It is, of course, possible that the Rav thought that we must adopt a wait-and-see approach and that it was too early to decide the nature of the

---

[24] "*Al Ahavat ha-Torah u-Ge'ulat Nefesh ha-Dor*," in *Be-Sod ha-Yahid ve-ha-Yahad*, pp. 424–25. The state is "insulated by the sanctity of the Land" (p. 430).

[25] Ibid. p. 430.

[26] Ibid.

young state. And, indeed, more than he wanted to issue a halakhic ruling on the matter, he wanted to influence what would happen and educate towards the future. But perhaps the fact that he pushed off the decision to the future says more than anything else. Did he act with sober patience, did he truly think that it was too early to decide that we are dealing with a secular, a-halakhic state, or was he simply unable to deny the historical and emotional significance of a Jewish state?[27] In any event, the Rav did not despair. He believed "that there is a silent demand on the part of thousands and ten thousands . . . to draw them near to the ultimate sources of man's consciousness of existence—the belief in a living God . . . The community's repentance will materialize tomorrow or in the future."[28]

## III

It seems that in another area as well a distinction can be made between Rabbi Soloveitchik's approach and Religious-Zionist thought. A fundamental and widespread assumption in Religious-Zionism—from Rabbi Reines, on the one side, to Rabbi Kook, on the other—is the acceptance of "the problem of Judaism," that is to say, the assertion that Judaism itself is in need of invigoration, even radical reformatory changes. "The problem of Judaism" parallels the "Jewish problem," and by this I refer not to the deplorable physical situation of the Jewish people in the historical Diaspora but to the social and economic wretchedness that also demanded internal reform. These ideas, which apparently adopted the Enlightenment critique, combined with the recognition of the mass abandonment of religion and Jewish identity. Zionism was supposed to cure all these ailments. On the one hand, the return to normal worldly-political existence, with all that this implies, was expected to instill a new spirit into Judaism and to repair the unsound social structure of the nation. On the other hand, the very

---

[27] In this entire discussion, the Rav did not invoke the category of "covenant of fate," but rather he conducted the discussion solely in terms of "covenant of destiny" (*Five Addresses*, pp. 141–43).

[28] "*Al Ahavat ha-Torah u-Ge'ulat Nefesh ha-Dor*," p. 432. This connects, of course, to "faith in the people of Israel," a motif that the Rav developed at length in his homilies on repentance.

national-Zionist aspiration was already a sign of return—first to the
nation and later to the faith. There is no need to point to the presence
of these motifs in the writings of Rabbi Kook. Regarding Rabbi Reines
as well, Dov Schwartz has determined that "the perception of Zionism
as a penitential movement is prevalent in the Rabbi's writings."[29]

These motifs are alien to Rabbi Soloveitchik. First of all, he did not
share the gloomy assessment that finds expression in the phrase, "Judaism's problem." He gives no indication that he felt that Judaism—that
is, halakhah and Jewish belief— suffer from an internal problem or essential deterioration. According to him, there is no fundamental problem whatsoever in classical Judaism. The Rav said, for example, that the
Brisker method of Talmud study brought about a serious intellectual
advance and even prepared Judaism to compete with the Western intellectual world; a sign that the Bet Midrash was in need of serious repair,
in his opinion. He even spoke about the important spiritual contribution of Hassidism. But this is a far cry from an all-embracing judgment in the spirit of "Judaism's problem." Neither the Jewish faith nor
halakhic practice require essential repair, in his opinion. So too he saw
no need or room for a moral transformation in Judaism like that which
Zionism was supposed to lead. You might say that he himself proposed
such a process, for example, when he promoted modern values, such
as creativity. But surely the Rav himself would not accept such an ap-
praisal; rather, he would argue that he is the loyal mouthpiece of tradition at its best.

The Rav did not think that Judaism is in need of urgent resuscita-
tion. This being the case, he found no legitimacy, spiritual majesty, or
hidden power in movements or individuals who wrestled with the laws
of the Torah. He did not perceive the shift to secularism as an idealistic
rebellion against the deficiencies of tradition or as a necessary attempt
to reach moral and religious levels that are beyond the reach of the Torah, as it is understood today or as it may be understood by its steadfast
students. According to him, what is needed is further study of that
which exists, not its uprooting. One must investigate halakhah and
understand its foundations rather than expect to rise above it.

---

[29] Dov Schwartz, *Etgar u-Mashber be-Hug ha-Rav Kook*, p. 221. The Netziv, as well, saw Hibbat
Zion as a display of repentance (Luz, "*Gevulot ha-Sovlanut*," p. 57).

I also do not find that the Rav expressed himself in the spirit of the Enlightenment-Zionist social criticism. He found nothing wrong with the social stratification or occupational diversity of the Jewish collective, with the fact that Jews are not found in certain professions or that they do not work the land. It is possible that he would have cast the responsibility for the situation on the countries in which they lived. In any event, he did not see in the situation that was created an essential blemish that adversely affected the nature of the Jew in the Diaspora, and he did not look forward to the improvement that Zionism would bring in this area. In general, he did not scorn the Galut (exilic) aspects of a Jew, except for the pain over a Jew's inability to defend himself and his family in a respectable manner.[30] He knows nothing of degenerative Galut traits, and accordingly he does not await the "new Jew."

Without a doubt, the Rav recognized the mass abandonment of religion and the assimilation eating away at the body of the nation. But he did not see Zionist activity as "repentance." I do not find in his writings the argument that already with the Jew's return to his national consciousness ("covenant of fate"), he has returned to his Judaism,[31] or that national repentance is a way-station along the route to full repentance. It is possible that this stemmed from his immediate and realistic experience with secular Zionism and its spokesmen; perhaps what could be seen in the 1950s could not have been seen in the 1920s. In any event, Rabbi Soloveitchik did not share the approach that saw in the establishment and building of the state a moment of Jewish spiritual actualization, sort of the beginning of a movement that restores its sons to their spiritual home.

The Rav was, indeed, of the opinion that the establishment of the State of Israel in the aftermath of the Holocaust prevented total national despair, the alienation of the Jewish masses from their national identity. There was no other answer to the gloom that came after the Holocaust, to the challenge to the desire to continue to be Jews but the establishment of the state, and it held the national body together. He also spoke in a more expansive manner about the role of the state

---

[30] *Fate and Destiny*, pp. 32–33.

[31] But see "Even the new secular settlement . . . acquired rights not only in the Land of Israel, but also in the Lord of Israel—howbeit indirectly and unconsciously" (Ibid,, p. 22).

in the formation of Jewish self-consciousness. In a certain sense, he expressed in homiletical terms the well-known sociological thesis that identification with the State of Israel effectively served for American Jewry as a substitute for traditional religious identification, though he saw in this an act of Providence, just as he defined the establishment of the state and its survival in those early years as a miracle, a wonder, an act of Divine grace.[32] "God decided in accord with Joseph against his brothers."[33] More than that: "Redemption was born."[34] It seems to me, however, that this "redemption" is the redemption of rescue from trouble and not the redemption of the end of days.[35]

## IV

Though the Rav's Zionist perspective is not messianic, there is a passage in his writings that introduces a measure of ambivalence to this assertion. This passage does not describe what is, but rather what could have been or perhaps what still can be. It is not a description of the real situation, but a metaphor—a metaphor that the Rav uses for the establishment of the State of Israel. The reference, of course, is to what is said about the lover's turning to his beloved in "Kol Dodi Dofek." The lover knocks on his beloved's door, but she is remiss in opening it, and the lover continues on his way. The Rav read this story as an allegory about God's emergence from the state of concealment in which He had

---

[32] *Fate and Destiny*, pp. 29–31. The Rav opens there with a description of "the era of self-concealment (*hastarat panim*) at the beginning of the 1940s," at a time when "the impulse to flee from Judaism and from the Jewish people reached a new height." But he continues in a slightly different direction. In any event, he emphasized the contribution of the state to the stabilization of the Jewish identity at the end of the 1940s, at a time when despair was on the rise. Of course, the entire article was written in the shadow of the Holocaust. See also: *Five Addresses*, p. 170.

[33] *Five Addresses*, p. 36.

[34] *Fate and Destiny*, p. 26–27.

[35] Regarding the fluidity of the term "redemption" see Efrayim E. Urbach, *Hazal: Pirkei Emunot ve-De'ot*, Jerusalem: Magnes Press, 5729, pp. 590–92. Of course, the influence of the homiletical style and situation on the person delivering the *derashah* must also be taken into account. For another sense of the term "redemption" in the Rav's writings (actually in an oral *derashah*), see Moshe Idel, "*Defusim shel Pe'ilut Go'elet bi-Yemei ha-Beinayimi*," in Zvi Baras (ed.), *Meshihiyut ve-Eskatologiyah: Kovetz Ma'amarim*, Jerusalem: Merkaz Zalman Shazar, 5744, p. 278.

been found since the period of the Holocaust; the knockings are the signs that He gave His people through the establishment of the state.

The Rav describes at length the opportunity missed by the beloved, and he wants us to understand that a similar lost opportunity threatens the Jewish people that is too lazy to answer the historical knocking of the establishment of the state. This is the way he describes that moment:

> The great moment that she had looked forward to with such impatience and longing . . . the realization and attainment of their aspirations and hopes . . . complete fulfillment . . . her heart's longings.[36]

On the level of the story of the lover and his beloved we fully understand the intention. But what is the meaning of expressions like "realization of hopes" and "full actualization" when we move from the allegory to reality? If the context is what is happening to the Jewish people by way of Divine Providence in the modern period, it turns out that we are describing the nation as standing at the doorstep of the end of days in the period of the messianic redemption. The allegory describes what could have happened but did not happen. The beloved did not respond to her beloved's knockings in time. But to what is the Rav alluding? Let us not forget that in contrast to what is hinted at here, the concrete-historical content of the "knockings" themselves were far from being messianic!

In contrast to the allegorical beloved who did not respond to the knockings of her beloved, who then turned away and was gone, the situation is different regarding the beloved—the people of Israel in the twentieth century:

> He has already been knocking for more than eighty years, and has not yet been answered in proper fashion. Nevertheless, he continues to knock . . . Oh, that we not miss the opportunity![37]

---

[36] *Fate and Destiny*, pp. 23–24.

[37] Ibid. p. 367.

The Jewish people, as opposed to the beloved in the allegory, can still respond to the lover and attain—what? "Realization of hopes" and "full actualization," with all that these expressions mean? Is this what the Rav had in mind? This interpretation is tempting but does not accord with the rest of what he says about Zionism, including what he says in "Kol Dodi Dofek." It seems that we will not be far from the truth if we assume that the Rav was carried away here in his homiletical enthusiasm and in his fervent desire to encourage the American religious community to respond to the challenge that Providence set before it, this in light of that community's disappointing response, as the Rav saw it, to the establishment of the state.

# Letters on Public Affairs

The written corpus left by Rabbi Joseph B. Soloveitchik deals with ideas, as expressed in halakhic and philosophic writings and in public talks or lectures. Until recently, one might have thought that statement to be accurate and that no surviving writings reflected the Rav's private or public life. That remains the case for the most part when it comes to personal and biographical matters; except for his students' reminiscences, we still have only the occasional autobiographical fragment appearing in a eulogy or article. Such fragments can be found as well between the lines of his halakhic correspondence, most of it exchanged with his father, R. Moshe (published as *Iggerot ha-Gerid Ha-Levi* [*Letters of the Ga'on, Rabbi Joseph Dov*], *5674–5701*[1]); they offer an occasional peek, subordinated to other matters, into his personality. As for the public sphere, we knew until now of only one article that dealt relatively broadly with interreligious dialogue, and we could ascertain his positions on political and Zionist issues from his lectures.

The publication in 2005 of *Community, Covenant, and Commitment,* edited by Nathaniel Helfgot,[2] has partly filled this gap, at least with respect to Rabbi Soloveitchik's public activities. We have here a collection of letters and documents from the Rav's pen, telling of his concrete actions in the context of American Orthodox Judaism and of his opinions on matters of concern within Jewish public life. In some instances they provide an entirely new perspective; in others, they

---

[1] Riverdale, NY, 5601

[2] R. Joseph B. Soloveitchik, *Community, Covenant, and Commitment: Selected Letters and Communications of Rabbi Joseph B. Soloveitchik*, ed. Nathaniel Helfgot (Jersey City, NJ: KTAV Publishing House for the Toras HoRav Foundation, 2005). Parenthetical page references in the present chapter are to this book.

provide new data confirming what was already known (or assumed); in still others, they show the practical face of a coin whose theoretical side has been long known. They also shed new light on the problems that religious Judaism was coping with at that time and place and the general lines of the Rav's practical and political thought along the entire front (and I use the military metaphor advisedly). These writings also tell something of the Rav's standing within the American Jewish community of the time. A substantial portion of the material in the book has appeared before, though not in English and not in easily accessible forums. As far as I know, the book has not yet been subjected to scholarly review.

Two additional factors make this a timely collection. First, the Rav's essay *Ish ha-Halakhah* often is cited as proof that he viewed the halakhah as the realm of the a priori, impervious to social reality, and as subject to a method partaking more of mathematics than of the human sciences. (Criticism of that approach seems to have increased following the publication in 1983 of Lawrence J. Kaplan's translation of the work, *Halakhic Man.*[3]) But that reading of *Ish ha-Halakhah,* taken alone, can afford a one-sided picture, for the Rav's halakhic involvement in public affairs was reasonably well known.[4] In any case, it is the Rav's own writings on public affairs that can provide the best illustration of his encounter with these matters—an encounter recognized by the author himself to have had an authentic halakhic component. Moreover, one can sometimes find in these documents a constructive interaction between halakhic positions and extra-halakhic values and concepts—at least on the explanatory plane if not on the substantive. On the one hand, the Rav might incorporate historical or philosophical moments into the presentation of his position; on the other, he might soften the halakhic data (or smooth their edges). At the same time, he might sometimes propose a purely halakhic solution to a social or communal problem, translating the halakhic concepts to meet the needs of the hour without sacrificing their force or original meaning.

---

[3] Philadelphia, 1983.

[4] For another work dealing with R. Soloveitchik's communal and educational activities, see Seth Farber, *An American Orthodox Dreamer: Rabbi Joseph B. Soloveitchik and Boston's Maimonides School* (Hanover, NH, 2004).

Second, since the Rav's death in 1993 (indeed, beginning with the eulogies at his grave), there has been a growing dispute over his cultural legacy and his personality. The dispute pits those who account for his modernistic vision and his openness to general learning as post-facto (*be-di'avad*) submission to the needs of the hour against those who see these traits as authentic aspects of his identity.[5] It may be naïve to expect a collection of the sort here presented to shed enough light on the question to resolve it; still, the hope endures.

# I

A small but, to my mind, particularly interesting portion of this material shows R. Soloveitchik in direct interaction with the gentile world. I am not referring here to the analysis of interreligious dialogue, an analysis directed toward the Jewish community (though it may well have reached gentile eyes as well) in an effort to guide it in its relationships with non-Jewish actors and institutions. Material of this sort certainly can tell of the Rav's opinions with respect to the gentile world, but its direct addressee is Jewish, not gentile. The Rav, however, was also called upon to represent the normative Jewish world before non-Jewish players.

One outstanding and interesting incident arose out of Cornell University's request that the Rav clarify the Jewish position regarding use of the human form (that is, representations of biblical figures) in the decorative windows of an interfaith center meant to be used for both Jewish and Christian worship (3–11). The request came from Professor Konvitz (the son of a *rav talmid hakham* and a man of strong Jewish identity), who served as the Jewish representative on the committee in charge of the project, but Konvitz made clear that the response would be directed to the president of the University and to the center's donor. According to the book's editor (p. xvi), the president of Cornell had agreed to abide by the Rav's determination—a surprising phenomenon in its own right. The Rav's response

---

[5] For an overview of the matter (from a particular perspective), see Lawrence J. Kaplan, "Revisionism and the Rav: The Struggle for the Soul of Modern Orthodoxy," *Judaism* 48(1999): 290–311. See also Kaplan, "The Multi-faced Legacy of the Rav, *BDD* 7 (1998):51–85.

is outstanding for its candor, its readiness to integrate philosophical and historical factors into its normative analysis, and its side-stepping of issues likely to generate perplexity.

The Rav begins by declaring that he cannot base his response on formal halakhah but must look as well to "central historical realities with their deep-seated philosophical meaning. . . . Such an approach is not a novelty in the history of the halakhah" (4). But why include all this? He begins—in a letter to the president of Cornell University!— with a summary but reasonably complete review of the talmudic attitude toward graphic representations of various sorts. That leads him to a passage in tractate *Avodah Zarah,* from which one can only conclude that the greatest of the *amora'im* permitted the presence of a noncultic human statue in a synagogue and that this teaching can be seen as normative. (The reader here sees the "teacher"—the *melammed,* as the Rav liked to call himself—in action. He could have forgone this entire analysis, had he not wanted both to teach Torah and to present the subject as frankly and directly as possible. Or might he have been worried that the addressee would check up on him or receive a permissive opinion that relied on this source?) Accordingly, this source provides a basis for ruling permissively. But the Rav then goes on to find that Judaism historically did not act in accord with this view and, as a practical matter, forbade the presence of human images in the synagogue. That approach is documented starting in Second Temple times, was consistently followed in the synagogues built in Christian Europe, and remains the practice to this day.

Here, the impact of Christianity proves decisive. In the Christian milieu, the Rav argues with outstanding cultural sensitivity, every human figure found in a cultic site instantly becomes a cultic figure—a consequence of the basic Christian belief in Jesus as a man-god and the view of the person in general as made in God's physical image.[6] Moreover, the artistic execution, even if limited to "suitable" biblical figures such as Abraham and Moses, will necessarily reflect the Christian ideal. These circumstances are quite different, then, from those of Babylonian synagogues in Talmudic times (6–8). The Rav describes

---

[6] Note that the Rav does not take the easy way out, which would have been to argue simply that the presence of human forms identifies the place as non-Jewish.

the process without casting any aspersions on Christian belief; at the same time, he emphasizes the profound theological gap that he sees between the two religions. His treatment here of the halakhic sources, I believe, provides not only an example of his deference to the tradition as actually practiced but also an illustration of his comment that when he decides a halakhic issue, he has "always been guided by a dim intuitive feeling which pointed out to me the true path" (276) and that "my inquiry consisted only in translating a vague intuitive feeling into fixed terms of halakhic discursive thinking" (25). That is so even though the argumentation here is far from halakhic, as the Rav himself acknowledges.[7]

But now, in concluding the piece, the Rav takes an unexpected and undiplomatic turn. He evidently had become aware that the decision to construct the multi-faith center had already been made and was no longer under discussion. Nevertheless, he adamantly expresses his opposition to the entire project. Here, in a letter written in 1950, the Rav already presents the essential elements of the perspective on interreligious dialogue that became clearer in the early 1960s with the publication of "Confrontation."[8] That perspective was built upon, among other things, the premise that each religion is fundamentally different from the others, though not on that account invalid. In the case at hand, he argues (8–10), the differences preclude the construction of a shared place of worship, for architecture and the disposition of space necessarily reflect a culture and a concept of the world. In that sense, Judaism and Christianity represent different and separate concepts of the religious experience, and bringing them together in a common building necessarily entails denial of one in favor of the other. The right of each religious culture's existence dictates that each be respected and given its own living space—a point that continued to characterize the Rav's teaching on interreligious dialogue throughout his life. It is noteworthy that the Rav manages to deny the legitimacy

---

[7] The Rav would look to the *midrash* that tells that Joseph mustered the fortitude to resist Potifar's wife's advances when he saw the image of his father's face in the window. It was not the normative rule that proved decisive but the vision of the ideal figure.

[8] Joseph B. Soloveitchik, "Confrontation," *Tradition* 6, 2 (1964): 5–29. Available at www.traditiononline.org.

of a shared house of worship for Jews and Christians without even hinting at the possibility that Christianity has the status of idolatry. It is hard to know whether to attribute that to the letter having been addressed to the (Christian) president of Cornell University or to some more fundamental approach. Either way, his raising a question about the very establishment of the center—a decision that had already been made—requires explanation. It seems to me that the Rav did not want to leave the impression—for his time or for the future—that he supported, even indirectly, the establishment of an interfaith center that would be used as a place of worship for both Jews and Christians. In a certain sense, perhaps, the Rav may base the unbridgeable cultural gap between the religions on an unstated premise that the religion at issue has a questionable theology; but I offer that conjecture hesitantly because there is also a basis for concluding otherwise.

It is hard to avoid the impression that this entire discussion—both the question at its center and the conceptual world invoked in the response—could come about only thanks to a certain American sociocultural environment. The same may be said of the Rav's letter on whether Jewish charitable organizations were obligated to do "their part" in taking in children abandoned on New York's streets, children who, in general, were automatically turned over to Protestant and Catholic organizations. (It should be noted that the question was not posed by an Orthodox agency.) Here, too, the Rav begins with a concise and abstract halakhic summary, but he chooses to rule in accord with more comprehensive halakhic guidelines—indeed, circumventing the sources that first seemed pertinent—and concludes by transforming the halakhic data into ideological terms. The preliminary halakhic discussion considers *Mishnah Makhshirin* 2:7 ("If one finds a cast-off infant—if most of the populace is gentile, [the infant] is gentile; if most of the populace is Jewish [the infant] is Jewish") and shows— through a characteristic halakhic analysis that does not shy away from such complex issues as whether and how halakhah should assess probabilities in cases of factual doubt—that despite the temptation to rely on this *mishnah,* it is not really relevant in our case. That is because its epistemological limitations—that is, its reaching a decision on the basis of which group is in the majority—makes it applicable only when dealing with more trivial issues, such as returning lost property or eating improperly slaughtered meat. In short, "the principle of majority is not applicable in cases of life and death" (17). In this case, the Rav argues, the halakhah should be determined on the basis of two other considerations: (1) the duty to save a Jewish child from being raised in another religion, something as important as avoiding mortal physical danger; and (2) the applicability of that duty even to a child whose Jewish identity is cast in doubt. It should be noted that despite the Rav's confident and unambiguous presentation, we are dealing here with determinations that are by no means simple, as the Rav himself suggests (certainly insofar as violation of the Sabbath provides an added dimension with respect to the obligation of rescue). Examination of the issue and all the pertinent sources can teach us much about the complexities of halakhic decision-making.[9]

At the end of his response (21), the Rav rejects the possibility of relinquishing these children—and not only to avoid "complications that might arise on the level of public relations." Waiving Jewish rights in this area would "be an admission of a feeling of inferiority and skepticism concerning the worth of our great and ancient faith." Moving here beyond the formal halakhic framework, the Rav declares—in rhetoric approaching a call to sanctify God's Name—that such a waiver would run contrary not only to the fundamentals of halakhah and the tradition but also to human dignity. Transcendent universalism does not warrant renouncing the Jewish sense that our faith is preferable to all others; and while we may not impose our

---

[9] For a summary overview, see *Shulhan Arukh, Orah Hayyim* 306:14 and 328:10; Maimonides, *Mishneh Torah, Hilkhot Issurei Bi'ah* 15:26 and Rabad, R. Moshe ha-Kohen and *Maggid Mishneh* ad loc.; *Shulhan Arukh, Even ha-Ezer* 4:34, Rama ad loc., and the commentary of the Vilna Ga'on ad loc; Nachum Rakover, *Mattarah Mekaddeshet et ha-Emza'im* [The End Sanctifies the Means] (Jerusalem, 2000), 261–92 (violation of the Sabbath to save one from converting). It should be noted that this subject—preventing conversion at the price of Sabbath desecration—is of the sort likely to generate, in addition to written legal sources, an oral tradition reflecting accounts of actual incidents. For a contemporary discussion showing the complexity of the issue, see Shaul Yisraeli, *Havvat Binyamin* 1 (Jerusalem, 5752 [1991–92]), sec. 14 ("*Ha-aliyyah mi-Rusiyyah ve-gidrei pikkuah nefesh*"). The Rav's position on the issue draws on that of R. Hayyim; see Aharon Lichtenstein, "*Mah Enosh*: Reflections on the Relations Between Judaism and Humanism," *The Torah u-Madda Journal* 14 (2006–7): 29 and 57, n. 132.

faith by force, neither may we surrender its children (even if their Jewish identity is in doubt) to other religions.

At this point, though, the Rav adds a surprising note: the foregoing statement is true not only of Judaism. Every religion is permitted, even bound, to take that same view of the religious experience it offers. "Religious tolerance asserts itself in the knowledge of the existence of a variety and plurality of God-experiences and in the recognition that each individual is entitled to evaluate his great unique performance as the most redeeming and uplifting one" (21–22). This effort to strike a balance between insisting on respect for Judaism and taking care that the respect not come at the expense of denigrating other faiths is something we will encounter again. Is it simply the product of pragmatism and of the survival instinct, or does it flow from a positive assessment of faith in general in a secularized world that challenges it? (Recall that the letter was not sent to a non-Jewish agency; its addressee was the head of a Jewish charitable organization and an alumnus of Yeshiva University.)

Another public issue, likewise involving both internal and external considerations, arose in 1951, during the Korean War. The United States military requested that Jewish religious institutions provide a quota of rabbis to serve as chaplains, but the call by Yeshiva University for volunteers from among its alumni failed to produce an adequate response. It was then suggested that the Yeshiva University Rabbinic Alumni/ Rabbinical Council of America require service by imposing significant sanctions on those who declined, and R. Soloveitchik was asked to rule on the propriety of doing so. Once again, the Rav began his response with a methodological pronouncement, this time longer and more detailed; it included a two-fold statement of reservations about the "objective" model of halakhic decision-making. First, every intellectual activity (including even aspects of natural science) combines formal components and human/intuitive components; in our case, he declared, his intuitive inclination was to approve the project (24–25).[10] Second, one must

---

[10] "I cannot lay claim to objectivity if the latter should signify the absence of axiological premises and a completely emotionally detached attitude. . . . In all fields of human intellectual endeavor there is always an intuitive approach that determines the course and method of the analysis. . . . Hence this investigation was also undertaken in a similar subjective mood." For a historical-biographical perspective on these and other materials see Lawrence Kaplan, "From Cooperation to Conflict," *Modern Judaism* 30,1 (2010), pp. 48–68.

distinguish between (but ultimately combine) "pure halakhic formalism which . . . places the problem on an ahistorical conceptual level . . . [and] applied halakhah which transposes abstractions into central realities, theory into facts. . . . Under this aspect I gave thought not only to halakhic speculation but also to [the] concrete situation" (25).[11] It is likely—though not certain—that the intuitive component of the process pertained primarily to the practical decision. In any event, it is clear that the Rav was not about to adopt the "mathematical" model of the halakhic process so admired within certain segments of Modern Orthodoxy—a model envisioned as automatically spitting out halakhic solutions solely on the basis of objective expertise. (It must be acknowledged, of course, that the Rav's essay *Halakhic Man* provided intellectual raw material for that notion.[12])

Most of the forty-page response deals with a classic halakhic question: Is it permissible, on a weekday, for a person to put himself in a situation in which he will be required, at some future point, to desecrate the Sabbath or commit some other transgression? In dealing with the issue, the Rav relies, as would be expected, on the view of R. Zerahyah Halevi, who, in the twelfth century, issued the leading permissive opinion.[13] But this analysis, though clear and penetrating, does not answer the question as posed and fails to engage the key problem. This response, as a practical matter, deals with the situation of a Jew who wants to volunteer for military service, despite its halakhic challenges. But the question presented is rather different: Is it permissible (and proper) for some other agency—the yeshivah—to impose military service on its alumni, even in a case where the government itself has not drafted the rabbis? (Chaplaincy in the United States military was on a volunteer

---

[11] This sort of acknowledgement is unusual but not entirely unprecedented. Cf. Rosh's *Responsa* 32:5: "With respect to this captive I tried in all ways to find a basis for permitting her [marriage] but I have despaired of finding an opening."

[12] Note that the Rav would refer to his essay "U-Vikkashtem mi-Sham," before it was published, as a work whose subjectivity would complement the objective aspects of *Halakhic Man*.

[13] The full discussion deals with questions of compulsion and force, with the distinction between cases involving mortal danger and those where that element is lacking, and with the distinction between a transgression that is certain and one that is only possible. The rather superficial summary I provide here is adequate for my purposes, but study of the issue in its entirety would certainly disclose additional relevant points and uncover interesting dimensions of the Rav's halakhic and value-based thought.

basis; accordingly, the halakhic obligation to comply with governmental law [*dina de-malkhuta dina*] was not at issue.) To that question, the Rav wanted to provide an unambiguously positive answer.

Here, the Rav invokes an entirely different set of considerations, invoking both the pragmatic and the value-based. First, he warns that the failure of Orthodox rabbis to enter the military will abandon the field—by which he primarily means Jewish soldiers—to Conservative and Reform clergy. Second, he points to experience in the previous war suggesting that soldiers indeed turn to military rabbis in times of personal or normative crisis, and it is desirable that the rabbi in the field be equipped with traditional halakhic knowledge and commitments. Third, if the Orthodox rabbinate stands on the sidelines, the liberal rabbinate will seize the opportunity to characterize the Orthodox as indifferent and uncaring. Finally, that sort of situation would likely have a disastrous effect on the government's attitude toward Orthodox rabbis and institutions, starting with the military exemption granted to yeshiva students. That last consideration—and it is not my purpose here to praise the Rav's political instincts!—says volumes about the attitude of Jews toward the American government during the early 1950s. From there, the Rav moves on, almost naturally, to describe the responsibility of the Jewish citizen to his civil homeland: the duty to contribute to its defense and the duty to support the Jewish soldier—and, perhaps, the non-Jewish soldier as well—in the spirit of the exhortation by the warpriest to the ancient Israelite army according to Deut. 20:2–4 and in the spirit of Maimonides' comments about the purity of the military encampment (*Guide of the Perplexed* 3:41). The values underlying all this may draw on the Rav's determination that the "tradition . . . has always wanted to see the Jew committed to all social and national institutions of the land of his birth or choice which affords to him all the privileges and prerogatives of citizenship" (57).

## II

Some of the issues treated in these letters and documents pertain to how Orthodox Judaism and Orthodox Jews relate to other religious bodies and movements. Under this heading, I include interreligious dialogue and contacts with the Catholic Church before the issuance of the Vatican declaration on the Jews, Orthodoxy's relations with the Conservative movement and its rabbis, and (even!) the relations between Orthodox rabbis and non-rabbinic Orthodox agencies. On the face of it, these groupings seem quite different from one another: What does the Pope have in common with the leader of Mizrachi? Isn't the very equation of the two demeaning? I would argue, however, that they share a common element, notwithstanding the vast substantive divides between them. As a practical matter, others have already considered the parallel between the attitude toward other religions and the attitude toward other streams within Judaism; they include Prof. Reuven Kimelman and R. Aharon Lichtenstein (who uses the term "parallel" [hakbalah] in this context).[14] Fundamentally, the Rav sees in each of these contexts the need to strike a balance (which will differ from case to case, of course) between drawing closer and keeping one's distance, thereby setting the boundaries of cooperation and of estrangement. The obligation to join forces for purposes that are positive and nonthreatening must be weighed, on a case-by-case basis, against zealous preservation of one's identity in the face of factors that imperil it. There is no doubt that Judaism, particularly Orthodox Judaism, had ample reason to feel threatened during the fifties and sixties. At the end of the day, therefore, the Rav's willingness to draw closer is as deserving of attention as his inclination to keep one's distance— and that despite the fact that from a socio-historical perspective, he was seen by those drawn to him ("mekorevav," to use R. Lichtenstein's term), and even by his circle of followers, as tending to reject dialogue.

1. The most dramatic and far-reaching subject in this group, of course, involves the policies outlined by the Rav with respect to inter-religious dialogue in general and dialogue with the Catholic Church in particular. The subject has been treated before, especially in the Rav's own writings ("Confrontation" remains the fullest presentation

---

[14] Reuven Kimelman, "Rabbis Joseph B. Soloveitchik and Abraham Joshua Heschel on Jewish-Christian Relations," *Modern Judaism* 24, 3(2004): 251–71; Aharon Lichtenstein, "*Gevulot ha-Shittuf im ha-Zibbur ha-Kelali*" [Limits on cooperation with the general community], outline of a lecture before the Israel Orthodox Forum, October 8, 2007.

of his position) but also in interpretations written from diverse perspectives; to these must now be added the material in the present volume. Let me first note that the Rav, as we saw earlier, had crystallized his position even before 1950, and the encounter with the winds of change coming from the Vatican during the 1960s was not a factor in their formulation. The subject has recently been treated by Reuven Kimelman, who documented the Rav's concrete activities during the period of contacts between Jewish agencies and the Vatican in a way that permits cross-checking his ideological statements against his practical activities.[15] Looking back from an Israeli perspective, it is interesting to note that Israeli rabbis and intellectuals did not take part in the nascent dialogue. The Vatican may have preferred, for theological and political reasons, to avoid involving people who might be seen as representing a Jewish political entity; but the lack of Israeli participation may also be explained by the identity of the Israeli candidates for participation.[16] In any case, the central figures in the discussion that developed were Abraham Joshua Heschel on one side and Joseph B. Soloveitchik on the other. The Rav's reserved stance exerted influence within the Orthodox community and beyond but failed to persuade the Jewish community overall, and the sixties and seventies were a heyday of interreligious dialogue.

As many have already noted, the Rav's reservations about interreligious dialogue were grounded in two different arguments. First, he was concerned about the missionary impulse that, he believed, remained characteristic of the Church. Acknowledging that the impulse was legitimate from the perspective of Christian theology, the Rav did not call for its abolition or raise any complaints against it. He simply objected to Jews cooperating with it or willingly submitting to it. Perceiving a sociological environment in which the majority community had an advantage over the minority community, he believed it necessary to avoid a dialogue that would lead to a comparison between the religions—a

---

[15] See Kimelman, "Rabbis . . ."

[16] On the members of the group organized by the American Jewish Committee, see Kimelman, 253. At one point, there was an effort to bring in Dr. Chaim Vardi of the Israeli Foreign Ministry as the World Jewish Congress's official observer at the Vatican Conference, but it was rejected both by the Vatican and by Jewish agencies (257).

comparison that, at the end of the day, would blur and even breach the boundaries between them. I need not quote passages in which this stance is expressed, but let me stress that the reader of these materials must become sensitive to the code words used in them. The term "dialogue," for example, signifies not an academic seminar but a personal-educational-therapeutic encounter in which each side is expected to learn from the other and even to be transformed through internalization of the values imparted by the other. One who enters into a dialogue without being ready for this sort of transformation—to a greater or a lesser degree—is considered to be acting in bad faith. It is no coincidence that the term "dialogue" was widely used for interpersonal encounters in those days, when Martin Buber served not only as a philosophical inspiration but also as a psychological guide. In any event, the encounter premised on similarity is what gave rise to the Rav's fears, and he proclaimed his Jewish-existential dread.[17] On the one hand, he spoke his words proudly and fearlessly; on the other, they resonate with age-old Jewish anxiety. He was not making small talk when he went out of his way to inform Cardinal Willebrands, during one of their private meetings, that his mother kept him indoors during the Easter season, lest he be attacked on the street.[18] In short, the Rav thought that nothing good for Jews or Judaism could come from interreligious dialogue, though, as we shall see, he did not reject the Jewish-Christian encounter.

Second, the Rav posited a philosophical foundation for rejecting dialogue[19]—a foundation that had already been set in place in his 1950 letter to the president of Cornell. As mentioned earlier, he argued even

---

[17] "We are therefore opposed to any public debate, dialogue, or symposium concerning the doctrinal, dogmatic, or ritual aspects of our faith vis-à-vis 'similar' aspects of another faith community" (260). The Rav goes on to enumerate ten specific topics that may not be the subject of a comparative dialogue; they include monotheism and the trinity, the messianic idea, the Jewish attitude toward Jesus, the idea of the covenant, and so forth. Without making too much of it, it seems to me that his use of the word "public" is not coincidental. Cf. David Hartman, *Love and Terror in the God Encounter: The Theological Legacy of Rabbi Joseph B. Soloveitchik* (Woodstock, VT, 2001), 131–65. In any case, I find in the Rav's writings no willingness to compromise on the point.

[18] Kimelman, 267, n. 31, reported by Atarah Twersky, the Rav's daughter. The meeting took place in the mid- or late 1960s at the Rav's home in Brookline.

[19] See Daniel Rynhold, "The Philosophical Foundations of Soloveitchik's Critique of Interfaith Dialogue," *Harvard Theological Review* 96 (2003): 101–20.

then that every faith community has its own structure, forms of expression, and content, and that these cannot coexist within a single architectonic space. In the present document, he speaks not of physical space but of spiritual. There can be no shared spiritual discourse because when it comes to faith and religion, there is no common language—or if there is a common language, it will rapidly become clear that that the words in it have different connotations. The autonomy of faith means more than the autonomy of the religious phenomenon vis-à-vis historical and sociological categories; it means as well the autonomy of each religion vis-à-vis the others. Not only is Judaism uninterested in hearing what Christianity has to say; by rights, Christianity should be uninterested in hearing what Judaism has to say, for there is no correlation between them. Each faith community has its own legitimacy, autonomy, and intimacy. I noted earlier that the Rav discusses Christianity without touching on the question of its halakhic status as a monotheistic religion. It may be that his emphasis on the unbridgeable gap between religions (between religions in general, but, in the present context, between Judaism and Christianity) is effectively equivalent to tarring Christianity with the brush of idolatry, for it precludes any dealings with it—and in conditions of exile, one cannot hope for more.

Of the two rationales for rejecting interreligious dialogue, the second—the philosophical one—seems the more problematic, presenting both methodological and biographical difficulties. With respect to the former, we must recall that the article "Confrontation," known to us as the basic text rejecting interreligious dialogue, figures in Orthodox thought on an entirely different plane as well. Section II of the article declares that there is an obligation to participate, shoulder-to-shoulder with all humanity, in universal *tikkun olam* ("improving the world"), in both the technological and social realms. Quotations from this article appear in anything written by Orthodox thinkers about *tikkun olam*. It is easy to see that the Rav is painting too rosy—too American—a picture here, but that is not our present concern. The point is that this joint effort will likely involve the spiritual leadership of all mankind, Jews included, and it is fair to assume that these spiritual and religious leaders will think and speak in the religious terms that come naturally to them. In this declaration, the Rav wanted to ensure that this effort at *tikkun olam* would not be a purely secular enterprise; but doesn't that necessarily open a back door to interreligious dialogue?[20] In one of the documents here (261), the Rav tries to get around these difficulties lurking in the corner, and the reader must judge whether he succeeds:

> Jewish rabbis and Christian clergymen cannot discuss socio-cultural and moral problems . . . in agnostic or secularist categories. . . . We [rabbis and clergymen] evaluate man as the bearer of God's likeness. We define morality as an act of *imitatio Dei,* etc. . . . Even our dialogue at a socio-humanitarian level must inevitably be grounded in universal religious categories and values. However, the categories and values, even though religious in nature and Biblical in origin, represent the universal and the public—not the individual and private—in religion. . . . We are ready to discuss universal religious problems. We will resist any attempt to debate[21] our private individual commitment.

Just how firm and clear is this distinction between universal and specific? Does it lend itself to unambiguous application in practice? In any event, the presence of spiritual values, which are likely to promote common discussions among neighboring religions—even if the Rav does not recommend such discussions for their own sake—provides an opening.

Nor does the personal side of things—that is, the Rav's own intellectual and spiritual pursuits—necessarily suggest absolute exclusion of interreligious dialogue; the issue is more complex than that.[22] For one thing, there is the Rav's widely noted affinity to the thought of Karl Barth (to which we may add Søren Kierkegaard, Rudolf Otto, and Max

---

[20] On the basis of that understanding, R. Moshe Feinstein in fact asked the Rav to withdraw his "permissive ruling" allowing joint Jewish-Christian discussion on societal matters, a form of cooperation that R. Feinstein considered threatening, not only because of its religious content but also because of the social environment it fostered. See David Ellenson, "A Jewish Legal Authority Addresses Jewish-Christian Dialogue: Two Responsa of R. Moses Feinstein," *American Jewish Archives Journal* 51, 1–2 (2000): 112–28.

[21] Again, I note the term "debate" appearing at a critical point in the final sentence.

[22] My comments in this paragraph correspond to Kimelman's observations.

Scheler—not coincidentally, it seems, all Protestants); more recently, his affinity to the thought of Emil Brunner has become more evident.[23] The Rav himself thus was open to non-Jewish religious thought and found it valuable (though one can always say that this view pertains only to the "universal" aspect of such thought).

Likewise complex and subject to varied interpretations was the Rav's personal response to the openings offered by Catholicism during the 1960s. On the one hand, there is no question that he was firmly opposed not only to Jewish participation but even to Jewish presence at the discussions in Rome. According to one report, he used his conversation with Cardinal Willebrands to reject any possibility of interreligious theological dialogue; and he acted accordingly with any Catholic representative. Another report, however, tells that at one of their meetings he asked Willebrands whether Catholic theology could ever believe in the salvation of a Jew loyal to his faith—a very different position on theological dialogue. But what is most provocative is that the Rav's great essay "The Lonely Man of Faith" was first presented, in 1964, as a lecture before a Catholic audience that had gathered at St. John's Seminary in Brighton, Massachusetts. In that essay, the Rav affords extensive treatment to the concept of covenant, not only between Adam and Eve but also between the Jewish community and God. Covenant, as noted, was among the ten subjects on which the Rav rejected interreligious discussion. According to the Rav's family (specifically, Dr. Atarah Twersky, according to Kimelman), the article pertains entirely to the universal aspect of religion. If that is so, the theological wall that marks the scope of interreligious dialogue—as distinct from the sociological boundary—is neither so high nor so firm; and R. Lichtenstein has already noted the impact of context in general on the Rav's policies here.

There is, I want to suggest, another document that indicates the complexity of the Rav's approach to religious dialogue as a universal phenomenon. In the spring of 1955, he proposed a change in the

---

[23] In addition to the citations provided by Kimelman, see the chapter "Biblical Models" in this volume, where I consider as well how the Rav's treatment of the Adam and Eve stories differs from Barth's. On Brunner, see Alan Brill, "Elements of Dialectic Theology" in R. Solveitchik's View of Torah Study." In H. Kreisel, ed., *Study and Knowledge in Jewish Thought* (Beersheva, 2006), pp. 265–98.

course of study leading to rabbinic ordination at Yeshiva. Among other things, he suggested that candidates for ordination be trained in philosophy, especially philosophy of religion (pp. 96–97, 100–101). In that context, he argues that if Second Temple Judaism had been able to formulate its ethical principles in philosophical terms comprehensible to Jews and gentiles alike, Christianity would have been unable to claim that it had uncovered new religious horizons. It is noteworthy that the Rav here calls for religious discourse addressed to gentiles as well and laments its absence in the past. But he is speaking not only of the past, for the context of his comments is a practical proposal. Moreover, he portrays American culture (in contrast to European) as open to religious discourse and responsive to religious philosophic stimuli. He sums it up in these terms: "Unfortunately, the all-inclusive, dynamic halakhah has become completely divorced from this querying and questing and is not involved in this *Sturm und Drang* theological movement which is so characteristic of the American religious scene today." It is not my concern here, of course, to locate the sources for this characterization or to discuss the great value the Rav attached to the intellectual dimension of religious discourse. What is important for us is what this plea says about the person who uttered it. We certainly cannot conclude that the person speaking these words was encouraging the rabbis he ordained to go out and arrange theological dialogues with their local Christian priests. What we can infer is that the Rav yearned, personally, for a cultural environment in which Judaism partook of shared spiritual-theological discourse with everyone (non-Jewish clergymen included) who engage in that sort of discourse—all as part of its integration into the American experience and ethos. That yearning evidently had no effect on his formulation of public policy, but it resided within in his heart.

2. Among the pressing intra-Jewish problems of those years was the relationship among the various Jewish streams and, in particular, the attitude of the Orthodox stream toward the others. We can here identify two leading issues: the need for a *mehizah* (partition) and/or separate seating for men and women in the synagogue, and the participation of Orthodox rabbis in umbrella organizations that included Conservative and Reform rabbis as well, such as the

Synagogue Council of America and the New York Board of Rabbis. On the first issue, the Rav's position was forceful and unambiguous. His dramatic ruling, renewed each year at the pertinent time in the American press, called on Jews to forgo hearing the shofar on the Rosh Hashanah if hearing it would require their presence in a synagogue having no separation between men and women.[24] It is as if he saw the issue as nothing less than the battle for the survival of Torah Judaism in the United States. His position on the second issue—Orthodox participation in umbrella organizations—was more nuanced, however.

Here is one treatment of the issue, excepted from an interview with the Rav (145–46):

When we are faced with a problem for Jews and Jewish interests toward the world without . . . then all groups and movements must be united. . . . In this realm we must consider the ideal of unity, as a political-historical nation, which includes everyone from Mendes-France to the "old-fashioned" Jew of Me'ah She'arim. . . . With regard to our problem within [the Jewish community], however—our spiritual-religious interests such as Jewish education, synagogues, councils of rabbis—whereby unity is expressed through spiritual-ideological collectivism as a Torah community. . . . Orthodoxy cannot and should not unite with such groups which deny the fundamentals of our *weltanschauung*. . . . The fundamental difference in ideology and observance make such a unity impossible.[25]

---

[24] The present volume includes several documents that give voice to the Rav's unyielding position on the matter; see pp. 125–42. On the distinction between a mixed-seating synagogue and a synagogue with separate seating for men and women but no *mehizah* between the sections, see the Rav's statement to a court in Cincinnati, Ohio that was considering the matter, 129–31. The Rav also rejected Orthodox participation in the committee preparing a new translation of the Bible, on the grounds that the translation would not reflect the Oral Torah's understanding of Scripture (110–11). This should be compared with the materials following.

[25] Here, too, however, the Rav adds a more tactical rationale: "Too much harmony and peace can cause confusion of the minds and will erase outwardly the boundaries between Orthodoxy and other movements" (146).

He tells us, for example, that "I tore up . . . immediately" a "responsum . . . sent me on the question of grafting human bone tissue. . . . I refuse to deal with any halakhic essay . . . prepared by a representative of a group whose philosophy is diametrically opposed to Torah and tradition and which does not accept the authority of halakhah as a Divine and transcendental guide. . . ." (119). The distinction parallels the one developed by the Rav in his discourse "Kol Dodi Dofek" between the covenant of fate and the covenant of destiny, though it is here applied in the practical world. But it also parallels the attitude toward the broader non-Jewish world: as long as we are speaking of general social questions, we should work shoulder-to-shoulder with Christians; but once we are speaking of particular spiritual values, there is no possibility of cooperation.

Although these principles are quite clear, their application, naturally enough, is more problematic. The Rav uncompromisingly rejected synagogues that did not seat men and women separately, yet he did not insist—as far as I know—on excluding rabbis who served such synagogues from the Rabbinical Council of America. He repeatedly declined (151–57) to issue a response on the participation of the Union of Orthodox Jewish Congregations and the Rabbinical Council of America in an organization that included synagogues of all streams, citing "the hysterical climate" (155) in which the issue had been discussed in rabbinic circles. He did participate, as he said, on matters related to "Jewish interests"; for example, he represented American Jewry in its entirety (including all the religious streams and even secular Jewish bodies) before the United States secretary of agriculture with regard to supervision of kosher slaughter—a matter of great historical and practical sensitivity in the Diaspora.

On a personal level, the Rav maintained friendly ties with Conservative and Reform rabbis. At times, however, the ideological problem proved perplexing and discomfiting. I get that sense from his letter (125–27) regarding his participation in an event honoring a Conservative rabbi in Boston. He declares his long-standing friendship with the honoree, the respect he accords him and his wife, and his wish that he could respond positively to the invitation. Had the event been devoted solely to this individual, the Rav would gladly have added his name to the list of sponsors. But because the event was to celebrate as well the dedication of a new synagogue for the honoree's congregation, a synagogue without separate seating for men and women, the Rav would see his participation as affording tacit approval for that arrangement, against the dictates of his conscience. I doubt the Rav struggled much in coming to this conclusion, but I sense from his words that his need to respond in the negative resulted in an unpleasant situation for him. (It is, by the way, typical of the Rav that the Conservative rabbi's years of service in a mixed-seating Conservative temple [the term used by the Rav, also adopted by non-Orthodox Jewry of the time] did not disqualify him as a friend in the Rav's eyes.)

His impassioned rhetoric notwithstanding, then, neither of these two subjects was unambiguously resolved by the Rav. Looking back forty years later, R. Lichtenstein could sum up that "application of the distinction [between permissible and impermissible cooperation] was often flexible, and his statements were not always precisely consistent. The circumstances, the subject, the public—all left their mark."[26]

3. Let me add a third piece to this discussion of the Rav's attitude toward non-Jewish and non-Orthodox actors: his posture vis-à-vis non-rabbinic actors—laymen and organizations working on behalf of Jewish causes, including non-rabbinic Orthodox and Religious-Zionist bodies. Here, too, the Rav set boundaries and maintained a degree of distance. Loyalty to halakhah, as the Rav interpreted it, was the determinative standard, from which it followed that halakhists, and only they, were authorized to decide halakhic matters or matters touching on halakhah. It should be noted that the Rav had rigorous aesthetic and religious standards and rejected the trivialization and lack of coherence that marked various proposed liturgical innovations. In practice, he took a strongly conservative position on liturgical matters. Affirming the coherence of the halakhah and the deliberateness and authoritativeness of the liturgical formulations arrived at by the talmudic sages and their successors over time, he rejected various efforts to introduce new liturgical formulations or structures.

---

[26] This translation is by the translator of this chapter, Joel Linsider.

Even where a proposal did not warrant immediate dismissal, it would be wrong for the liturgy to respond hastily to the events of the day; in that regard the Rav would quote the talmudic account (*Shabbat* 21b) of the institution of Hanukkah: "in a later year they established them and made them into festival days"—they were established only after calm reflection. In short, the Rav was not much occupied with halakhic "dynamism"; and even when he acted in a way that effected changes, he portrayed the results he reached, in typically conservative fashion, as following from classical halakhah.

To take one example, he declined to introduce any reference to the Holocaust into the Passover Haggadah, whose structure, in his view, was based on a closed and self-sufficient liturgical logic that precluded reference to any historical tragedy other than the enslavement in Egypt. And if there was a need for liturgical recognition of the bicentennial of American independence, the task should be assigned by Orthodoxy to its rabbis, who would follow the guidance provided by the spirit of Jewish prayer, and not to nonreligious players (115–18). The Rav himself expressed his willingness to participate in such a task force, if it were established. He more or less characterized R. Shlomo Goren's proposal to recite Hallel on the night of Yom ha-Azma'ut as outrageous foolishness, and one can only imagine his reaction to the crazy-quilt of prayers proposed by the Israeli rabbinate for use on that night. His opposition to a proposal that the RCA disseminate liturgical material for Yom ha-Azma'ut prepared by the Mizrachi movement (123–24) manifests his sense that a rabbinic organization should never serve as the agent for some other body with respect to halakhic matters. The issue was not the amateurishness of the materials but the fundamental impropriety of the suggestion; rabbis should never give up their full measure of authority with regard to anything having a halakhic aspect. It is, simply, "below our dignity to serve in the capacity of a mailing agency for any group" (124).

But the Rav showed conservatism in liturgical matters even where he did not reject a proposal on halakhic grounds. He recommended that mourning for the victims of the Holocaust be incorporated into the Fast of the Ninth of Av—a widespread traditionalist position— but he did not look kindly on the writing (even by contemporary rabbis) of special dirges on the subject. He took that position even though the existing collection of dirges includes poems devoted to events other than the destruction of the Temple. At issue here, in effect, is not any halakhic prohibition but liturgical conservatism pure and simple—a conservatism grounded, on the one hand, in recognition of the careful formulation of the prayers that have come down to us and, on the other, in deference to the great figures who composed the prayers. But whatever its origins, the position is a conservative one.[27] Notwithstanding the widespread image of the Rav as "halakhic man," then, we find many cases in which he decided an issue in accord with the historical model that presented itself to him, that is, the conduct of the community of Israel and its great scholars through the ages as he perceived them—a sort of "image of his father's face in the window," as in the midrashic account of Joseph in Potifar's house. This trait gained explicit expression in the letter to the president of Cornell discussed earlier, as well as in his attitude toward liturgical innovations in memory of the Shoah.

## III

At this point, we should consider some characteristics that cut across specific issues. Two terms that appear frequently in the present volume are "dignity" and "respect." The Rav is very concerned that Orthodoxy has lost its dignity. He does not mean by this that it is insufficiently formal, nor is he referring to any lack of honor, of ceremonialism. On the contrary, he already discerned, early in the 1960s, that American Jewry had become disillusioned with the ceremonial sheen of organized religion, and he saw the beginnings of the search for less-established religions—though he certainly did not foresee the

---

[27] The Rav attacked this issue from various perspectives but always arrived at the same result. See, now, Joseph B. Soloveitchik, *The Lord Is Righteous in All His Ways*, ed. Jacob J. Schacter (Jersey City, NJ, 2006), 266–67, 289–301, 300–302, and index, p. 343, s.v. Holocaust. For an attempt to identify the Rav's position with Haredi thought, see Aryeh Edrei, "*Keizad Zokherim? Zikhron ha-Sho'ah ba-Hevrah ha-Datit u-ba-Hevrah ha-Hilonit*" [How to Remember? Memorializing the Holocaust in Religious and Secular society], *Tarbut Demokratit* 11 (2007):15, 43–44. And that is how his opinion is recalled by students and audience members; see Edrei, 15, n. 31.

emergence of New Age sensibilities (188). He was referring primarily to an absence of personal spiritual depth and to intellectual decline—tendencies that he saw in the public arena as well. One gets the sense that he regarded American Jewry, and Orthodox Jews in particular, as a spiritually and culturally enervated group, whether compared to the Jews of Western Europe or to those of Eastern Europe. In drawing those comparisons, to be sure, he had in mind the elites of those communities, but he believed no such elite existed in America. His students were talented and well prepared, but he decried their lack of historical (and religious) rootedness, their personal roughness, and their limited spiritual development. Accordingly, Orthodoxy needed to internalize the recognition that it represented a significant, venerable tradition and to act accordingly.

Another characteristic evident in some of the letters is the Rav's willingness to go forward on the basis of an existing situation, even if problematic. We saw one example in his readiness to confront the religio-cultural significance of the spiritual center to be built at Cornell, though not concealing his sense that it would have been better had the project never been conceived. An additional example, which I have not considered here, is his attitude toward establishing a medical school within Yeshiva University. On the one hand, he understood that the project would be a halakhic adventure, to say the least. He declares at the outset that he was not asked in advance about "the necessity and practicality of a medical school under the auspices of Yeshiva" (86). The question posed to him is only *be-di'avad* (post facto). And yet, he reminds us, all of life is *be-di'avad;* "it would have been preferable for man not to have been created, but now that he has been created. . . ." Accordingly, he considers the project to be a given; as such, the policy toward it should be one that blends respect and suspicion. On the one hand, one should recognize the great opportunities offered by the new institution for enhancing Orthodoxy's image, building bridges between the religious public and a medical community not known for holding the tradition in great esteem (he here refers to the writings of Y. L. Peretz and Sholem Aleikhem!) and promoting the welfare of the community. At the same time, one must take pains that any affront to halakhah be kept to a minimum. It seems to me that the

Rav's attitude toward Zionism similarly draws, at some points, on this same distinction between *be-di'avad* and *le-khattehilah* (pre-facto) and on his willingness to work on the basis of a situation as given.

# IV

The book includes materials on many other public issues, but I will conclude with some texts on a personal matter, namely, the give and take regarding the possible appointment of the Rav as Ashkenazi Chief Rabbi of the State of Israel following the death of Chief Rabbi Unterman in 1959. Some of this material has already been published, some not; in any case it is now gathered and presented in one place. A critical question, I believe, is the extent to which the reasons offered by the Rav for declining the appointment were, in fact, the only reasons. He begins one of the letters on the subject by noting that he is writing without taking into account the effects of his decision on his family and friends. We do not know how the Rav's wife reacted to the suggestion that they move from Boston to Jerusalem and that the Rav take on the role of Chief Rabbi.

The basic rationale articulated by the Rav was the political and public nature of the Chief Rabbi's role—two separate features of that role, both of which he shied away from. He had in mind both the Rabbinate's ties to the government in general and the intrigue within religious Judaism itself. (He told me that David Ben-Gurion had sent an emissary to assure him that if he agreed to be nominated for the job, he—Ben-Gurion—would ensure that he was elected. In reply, he told the emissary that it was precisely Ben-Gurion's ability to ensure who was elected Chief Rabbi of the State of Israel that kept him from accepting the office. The Rav alludes to this proposal in a May 1960 letter to Moshe Unna [191] but says he is not free to disclose the identities of the players in the episode.) He saw himself as a teacher of Torah and a thinker, and he had doubts about whether he would be able to maintain those roles while also serving as Chief Rabbi. He describes at length his informality, a trait ill-suited to the image of the Chief Rabbi current in Israel; he did not, in fact, dress as a rabbi or speak in rabbinic style. In America, too, he was called upon to play a public role, but the extent of that role was vastly smaller than what could be anticipated of the Chief Rabbi, as he well understood. His concerns strike me as eminently reasonable and perceptive. He envisioned a rabbinic ideal of study and spiritual leadership, and he doubted—with justification—whether he could carry it out, particularly given his weakened physical state following surgery for stomach cancer. While he indulged no illusions, he thought he could bring his learning and personality to bear on the nonobservant public in Israel, though he fully understood that the time was not ripe for a mass return to religion (185). One may ask whether his personality was well suited to playing such a role.

What is surprising in this exchange of letters is the seriousness with which the Rav entertained the possibility of serving as Chief Rabbi. A careful reading of the letters and interviews shows that he took a positive view of the proposal at the outset and even envisioned, in his mind's eye, how he would carry out the role (175): "I had decided to assume the spiritual burden of the nation." Among the changes he would insist on—and he thought about the stipulations—was the placement of (religious) education under the authority of the Chief Rabbi. That he be granted authority in the area of education was the only concrete demand he seems to have presented, and it is very characteristic of him. In his letter to Moshe Shapira he writes that he cannot respond positively "at the moment" (176); and while that phrase may have been added only out of politeness, it may also convey some interest in leaving the door open. He wrote to R. Reuven Katz that, at the outset, he "decided to listen to you and take up the burden of the great rabbinate" (177). And in his final letter to Unna, in January 1961, he sums up the situation by saying "regarding the issue itself, the air must first be cleared . . . and this cannot be done except through far-reaching changes in the election procedures for and the powers of the Chief Rabbinate" (194). The word "first" suggests a possibility of reopening the discussion, as unrealistic as that seems. But this is by no means clear, and it is entirely possible that he meant only to end the matter smoothly and pleasantly.

* * *

*Community, Covenant, and Commitment* includes documents and letters written by the Rav on other subjects, and much could be said about them as well. The present essay is by no means exhaustive. The reader will find, for example, units on education, on the "Who Is a Jew" question posed by David Ben-Gurion to Jewish sages, and more. Beyond its specific contents, the volume attests not only to the Rav's involvement and centrality in the life of the Orthodox community but also to the way in which he applied principles and commitment to those principles in dealing with issues arising in day-to-day life. Naturally, some of these issues have already become obsolete, but that is certainly not the case regarding the spirit and method applied in treating them. The final word in the title, "Commitment," is a modern term (and, perhaps, a modern concept), which, I believe, became prominent in its prevailing sense in existentialist thought; but the Rav used it extensively, as a code for what he demanded of those who heed his teachings. It accurately characterizes his own way even outside the world of the study hall.

More than anything else, the issues I have discussed here shed light on the image of the Rav as a public figure drawing on a deep spiritual heritage while confronting a new and changing world. I have included no sociological/historical discussion of the influence exerted on his contemporaries by the Rav, his positions, and his pronouncements, nor have I sought out the concrete background for those positions. Those inquiries require tools and knowledge different from those brought to bear on the present discussion.

# Biblical Models

Both "Kol Dodi Dofek" and "The Lonely Man of Faith" have by now been the subject of much discussion and exposition. These treatments, however, are almost always devoted to the substantive, ideological, dimensions of the work. Less attention has been paid to the fact that both these major essays are constructed around readings of a Biblical text.[1] We shall therefore devote our inquiry to the question of R. Soloveitchik's relation to these Biblical texts and, in part, to his relation to Biblical materials as a whole. How does he read these specific texts? Do these readings form a pattern, and can we then suggest anything about R. Soloveitchik's encounter with the Biblical narrative?

## I

R. Soloveitchik's presentation of Biblical interpretation differs radically from his study of rabbinic materials, that is Talmud, Maimonides, or the like. These will be taught as pure theory, or in religious terms, as fulfillment of the command to study and teach Torah. Such study is not necessarily intended as a response to any immediate need for normative guidance. It is, rather, a largely intellectual gesture, which may even court irrelevance. Naturally, though, it is always committed.

The Biblical explorations, on the other hand, are all topical. R. Soloveitchik has not published any independent Biblical studies, that is, studies that have as their goal the illumination of Biblical texts or episodes

---

[1] For an exception to this generalization, see the Hebrew essay of my late colleague, Pinchas Peli, "The Uses of Hermeneutics ('*Deruish*') in the Philosophy of J. B. Soloveitchik—Method or Essence," *Da'at* 4 (1980), pp. 111–28.

for their own sake. Rather, R. Soloveitchik reflects on the Bible in the context of his encounter with the current existential dilemmas of the Jewish people or individual.[2] So "Kol Dodi Dofek" deals with the situation of the Jewish people in the twentieth century against the backdrop of the Holocaust and the establishment of the State of Israel. And "The Lonely Man of Faith" deals with the forlorn situation of the man of faith in the modern, technological, world. In both cases, R. Soloveitchik's belief and hope are expressed in his reading of Biblical texts.

## II

The ostensible topic of "Kol Dodi Dofek" is the creation of the State of Israel. The talk was originally delivered as part of an Israel Independence Day ceremony, and R. Soloveitchik used the opportunity to celebrate the religious legitimacy of the Jewish state, declaring its emergence in the twentieth century to be the work of God's hand in history. Israeli schoolchildren, indeed, read the work as a classic of Religious-Zionism. As expected, R. Soloveitchik also treats of the Holocaust and its proximity to the creation of the State. The Biblical paradigm for these events is the experience of the Children of Israel in Egypt. At first enslaved and subject to gruesome genocidal torture, they are redeemed by God and led, if circuitously, to the Holy Land.

Yet it has always struck me that this restatement of twentieth-century Jewish history is not the real topic of the piece; indeed, it avoids the true problematic that the emergence of the state embodies. For the State of Israel is, primarily, a secular reality, and it graphically represents the secularization of Jewish peoplehood in the modern world. How can this be legitimate? Celebrated, indeed? The true topic of "Kol Dodi Dofek," then, is the character of the modern Jewish people, or, more precisely, the integration of this reality into the worldview of the believing Jew.

The key to an interpretation of contemporary Jewish existence is found, for R. Soloveitchik, in a reading of the book of Exodus. Slavery, Redemption, Sinai: these are the themes that shall illuminate

---

[2] This is true even for the Rav's recently published *Abraham's Journey*, eds. David Shatz, Joel B. Wolowelsky, and Reuven Ziegler (KTAV, 2008). See, p. 17.

contemporary Jewish existence. This move is made simultaneously with a maneuver that is characteristic of R. Soloveitchik's midrashic work—we shall also encounter it in "The Lonely Man of Faith"—but that may have been borrowed from his halakhic method. Simply put, R. Soloveitchik frequently discovers contrasting characteristics in ostensibly unitary or homogeneous topics. In our case, then, the topic at hand is the Jewish people (or, indeed, peoplehood in general). As R. Soloveitchik unpacks it, two primary—and contrasting—components come to the fore.

Briefly put, the identity of the Jewish people moves on two levels. The people's identity is forged by historical experience that is imposed by the Other who possesses the power to do so, and this experience is suffered by the Jew as object. But identity is also created when the people—as subject—appropriates its culture, goals, ideals, norms, and values. For R. Soloveitchik, both moments are covenantal. Both moments embody communal existence, and both moments invite commitment. The first is called the Covenant of Fate (*brit goral*); the second is called the Covenant of Destiny (*brit ye'ud*). The first covenant is present in the communal existence of Jews per se, secular or observant, inasmuch as they remain subject to the historical fate of their people. The second covenant is embodied in the existence of the community that is actively committed to Jewish belief and practice. This distinction does seem overly schematic at times; thus, even fated communal existence calls forth solidarity and even love—responses that frequently embody ethical and normative standards. This objection notwithstanding, though, R. Soloveitchik has adopted a typology that enables him to make sense of modern Jewish history, and that he can discover in his Biblical texts, as we shall see.

This dual covenant, R. Soloveitchik claims, is already present in the very coming into being of the Jewish people. The experience of slavery in Egypt is read as the archetype of the Covenant of Fate, as the people suffer the condition imposed upon them. In twentieth-century terms, Egypt is Holocaust, as the slave people become the pure objects of the will of others. Indeed, though Jewish peoplehood was chosen in modernity by many who abandoned Jewish faith, the Holocaust is a pure case of Jewish fate imposed totally by the Other, in almost mythological terms. Now, by placing the Holocaust experience at the very foundational moment of Jewish history—Egyptian bondage—R. Soloveitchik makes legitimate room in the structure of this history for those Jews who suffer the historical fate of Jewry—whoever they are. The Holocaust was suffered, of course, by secular, atheistic Jews no less than by believers. And so, national solidarity and identity cannot be restricted, even from the normative perspective of the believing community, to the traditionally observant.[3]

It is likely, then, that the existence of the secular Jew and his community provided the problematic that R. Soloveitchik undertook to confront in "Kol Dodi Dofek." But it must be emphasized that the Covenant of Fate does not accommodate that Jewry alone. Rather, R. Soloveitchik asserts that all Jewries have embodied both covenants, which are structural givens within Jewish existence. The Abrahamic family expresses the Covenant of Fate, for example (despite Abraham's strong Biblical association with a variety of Judaic ideals). A more powerful symbol of this covenant is circumcision: it is engraved in the very body and is subsequently inescapable, and it suggests the suffering attendant on the Covenant of Fate. Thus R. Soloveitchik claims that in the traditional ritual of conversion to Judaism, circumcision represents the entry of the new Jew into the body of his people, while immersion (*tevillah*) represents the commitment to the spiritual Sinaitic Covenant of Destiny, its norms and values. R. Soloveitchik doubtless notes that circumcision has remained a badge of Jewish identity even among many otherwise secular Jews.[4]

The Covenant of Destiny is embodied in Sinai, in the giving and acceptance of the Torah. At that point the people choose its identity, becoming the subjects of history rather than its object. Now, beyond group solidarity, the people is committed to a culture, an ethic, a structure of values, a code of behavior. In this reading of Exodus, the people of Sinai stand across a great divide from the people of Egyptian slavery. The Biblical text describes a group that moves from one point to the other fairly expectedly. But with his contemporary

---

[3] For a fuller discussion, see this volume's chapter "The Jewish People."

[4] *Fate and Destiny*, pp. 60–63.

agenda and typology, R. Soloveitchik implies that the move from Egypt to Sinai is a struggle, a creative moment that requires great resources of will.

The exodus itself now takes on a different character. Let us recall, now, that for R. Soloveitchik, this end of Egyptian bondage represents the physical rebirth of the Jewish people through the establishment of the State of Israel. This event, however, also marks the great hour of secular, nationalistic, Jewry. Both modern Jewish existence and the exodus experience it embodies become, therefore, mutually-reinforcing but ambiguous, multi-valent, realities.

The exodus from Egypt, dominated as it is by God, lends a transcendent significance to the establishment of the State, despite its secular origins. Indeed, R. Soloveitchik is even eager to apply the messianic verses of the Song of Songs to this event. Ethnic solidarity thus receives full legitimacy. On the other hand, R. Soloveitchik is extremely critical of secular Jewish existence, and sees it—in its pure forms—as a betrayal of Jewish destiny. More to our point, he must also see it—despite its very achievements and career—as a historically conditioned response, rather than as an embodiment of positive content and value. Paradoxical as it may seem, the exodus may also now be seen as the experience of a people who have not yet really chosen to commit themselves but are simply acted upon—if not by historical forces, then by God. Indeed, the people Israel will themselves complain in the desert that they were manipulated—if not shoved—into freedom.

The exodus experience—bondage, release, Sinai—is no longer a series of events relating to the creation of the people of Israel, and the story of this experience is not a historical document in the normal sense. Rather, it has become a narrative of Israel's formation, in all the possible senses of that term. For, R. Soloveitchik claims, the basic terms of Israel's formation—fate and destiny—remain encoded, as it were, in the very structure of its national existence.

Much of R. Soloveitchik's thematic, his terminology, and even his Biblical reading, parallels that of Martin Buber and, perhaps, was drawn from him or other European thinkers. Though traditional models exist as well, particularly in the writings of his great-grand-father, as I have pointed out elsewhere, it is difficult to overlook the Buberian materials. The Buberian discussion is set in his talk on "Nationalism" that was delivered in 1921 and appeared in very accessible form in 1936 as a chapter of *Zion als Ziel und als Aufgabe.* Buber distinguishes between "people" (*Volk*) and "nation":[5]

> . . . the concept "people" always implies unity of fate (*Schicksal*). It presumes that . . . throngs of human beings were shaped into a new entity by a great molding fate they experienced in common.

> A people becomes a nation to the degree that it grows aware that its existence differs from that of other peoples . . . conscious and active difference. . . . This consciousness is usually the result of some . . . inner transformation. . . . It is decisive activity and suffering . . . which produces a *people*. A *nation* is produced . . . [by] decisive inner change which is accepted as such in the people's self-consciousness . . .

This basic analysis is applied by Buber to Jewish existence:

> A great . . . event molded the Jews into a people. It was when the Jewish tribes were freed from the bondage of Egypt. But it required a great inner transformation to make them into a nation. In the course of this inner change, the concept of the government of God took on a political form . . . the kingdom as the representative of God . . .

Much is in Buber that we find in the later R. Soloveitchik: the fundamental, categorical, distinction of people and nation, fate and destiny; the objective-passive facticity of peoplehood as over against the subjective-active consciousness of nationhood; and even the playing out of these formative moments in Egypt and Sinai. There are differences too, to be sure, and these are also worth noting. In *his*

---

[5] I cite from the English translation, "Nationalism," in Martin Buber, *Israel and the World* (New York, 1948), pp. 217–18, 222. For discussion of R. Soloveitchik's traditional sources, see the materials cited "The Jewish People" in this volume.

Biblical reading, Buber sees the exodus as formative, rather than the Bondage: Buber spoke before the Holocaust; R. Soloveitchik, after. And, I surmise, R. Soloveitchik's covenant at Sinai is a rather different thing than Buber's "Kingdom of God." Yet there is one truly major difference, and that concerns the basic function of the two hermeneutics. Buber is concerned, in 1921, with the problem of noxious, pathological, nationalism. R. Soloveitchik is concerned with the creation of the State of Israel and the secularization of the Jewish people, its abandonment of its sacral identity. He is determined to make room for Jews who are not pious or even believers. But he also contends that the secular Jew and his state participate in a truncated Jewish existence, sharing Jewish fate but rejecting Jewish destiny.

# III

Formally, the hermeneutic structure of "The Lonely Man of Faith" resembles that of "Kol Dodi Dofek." Once again, a topic is analyzed through a double prism. Adam and Eve become the models for two distinct types of human person, indeed of two distinct forms of culture. Covenantal terminology and categories are, again, central to the argument. Here, too, R. Soloveitchik's concerns are deeply contemporary even as they engage the Biblical text. Finally, "The Lonely Man of Faith" opens up areas of reality that traditional Judaism often ignores or even rejects—much as "Kol Dodi Dofek" did in its own way. At the same time, "The Lonely Man of Faith" works much more closely with the Biblical narrative. Perhaps one could describe it as genuine hermeneutic, rather than as homily. It is, indeed, best compared with Karl Barth's treatments of the same Genesis materials in his *Church Dogmatics*—a comparison to which I shall return later.

The basic Biblical structure around which R. Soloveitchik builds his discussion is the double creation narrative and, more specifically, the twice-told story of the creation of Man and Woman. Rather than harmonizing away the distinctions between these texts, he pushes them to the limit, claiming that the author intended a wealth of meaning in each narrative and, especially, in the tensions and contrasts he introduced. Now, contrary to popular opinion, even the ancient Jewish sages knew full well that "the two accounts of the creation of man differ considerably." But the meaning of this phenomenon is not to be found "in an alleged dual tradition but in dual man, not in an imaginary contradiction between two versions but in a real contradiction in the nature of man."[6] This duality finds expression, moreover, on a number of interrelated planes, ranging from humanity's relationship with nature to the relations between the sexes.

Man and Woman of Genesis 1 are to "fill the earth and master it," to "rule the fish of the sea, the birds of the sky and all the living things that creep on earth." The image of God in humanity—following much Jewish exegesis and despite the current ecological debate—lies in our ability to dominate the environment, in what R. Soloveitchik calls (somewhat anachronistically) a technological mode of existence. Even the immediate blessing to the first pair that they "be fertile and multiply" is, in a sense, an environmental imperative and it is to this end—anticipations of Phyllis Bird?—that they are created "male and female." Taking this reading one step further, R. Soloveitchik insists that the human order thus constructed presages a utilitarian collective, but not a community of covenantally committed persons. The vision is functional, both as regards First Adam's relationship to nature and as regards the relationship between the sexes. And R. Soloveitchik notes that in contrast to the narrative in Genesis 2, there is no struggle, no failure, no search, no sacrifice, and no sin. First Adam does not taste defeat; technological man is a success.

Now it must be stressed that First Adam is an extremely positive figure for R. Soloveitchik. Technological man and woman fulfill a permanent, divine, imperative encoded in humanity; First Adam is the "majestic" person in R. Soloveitchik's terminology, terminology that draws heavily on Psalms 8. Much as with the Covenant of Fate in "Kol Dodi Dofek," R. Soloveitchik reads the Biblical history in a way that requires that the contemporary traditional community broaden its scope of concerns. In our case, he enthusiastically endows Western

---

[6] "The Lonely Man of Faith," p. 10.

scientific technology with the fullest acknowledgement Judaism could offer. (In the sixties, it is true, this demand may have seemed a virtual truism; but now, as the orthodox community grows increasingly insular, it has become surprisingly relevant and debatable.)

Yet despite this full embrace of First Adam, it is Second Adam (the Adam and Eve of Genesis 2) who takes center stage. First Adam always remains a basic component of the human person and culture, but Second Adam has axiological priority; the values he (or she) embodies, the experiences he undergoes, rank the higher. Second Adam is the "Lonely Man of Faith."

The fundamental problematic of Second Adam is encapsulated in God's introductory comment to the creation of Eve: "It is not good for Adam to be alone." In R. Soloveitchik's modernist version, God here introduces the basic thematic: there is something problematic, something not good, in Adam as thus created. This "aloneness," which quickly becomes "loneliness," is not merely a functional or even a psychological category. It is ontological.

Second Adam's relationship with nature is not successful or fulfilling. Genesis 2: 19—20 tells the story of Adam's unsuccessful search in the animal kingdom for a mate—a search that leaves him alienated and conscious of his basic loneliness: "And the man gave names to all the cattle and to all the birds of the sky and to all the wild beasts; but for Adam no fitting helper was found." Thus, it is only after Adam becomes conscious of his fundamental uniqueness and need that Eve will be created. But there is much more to the delayed creation of Eve. Second Adam—both male and female—is not only ontologically alone. The next phase of the narrative is equally significant: woman can be created only when an overpowering sleep falls upon man, and she is taken from his body. "This new companionship is . . . attained . . . through surrender and defeat."[7] R. Soloveitchik has been faulted for what some critics have seen as an exaggerated stress—for a Jewish thinker, especially—on the value of defeat and surrender. Here, though, the point is made in the context of meaningful human relations and communication, and it is difficult not to be impressed by the coherence of the hermeneutic with

---

[7] Ibid., p. 26.

personal reality. True, dialogic relationship requires, indeed, that Adam "give away part of himself," and true communication requires sacrifice. The contrast with the simultaneous and painless creation of First Adam is marked. Indeed, we ought note that Second Adam's loneliness describes not only the human void that can be filled by true companionship alone. It also characterizes the position of the fully human person and his community as he confronts technological civilization and the political culture of the collective. Second Adam is lonely even in the company of First Adam.

R. Soloveitchik makes one further major interpretive step. He insists that the relationship of Adam and Eve is dialogic and covenantal not only by virtue of its origins in the existential individuality of each person and their union. Since the Biblical narrative describes God as He who "summoned Adam to join Eve," one may see God as having committed Himself to them. R. Soloveitchik argues that God is Himself never outside the covenantal community, which is now a community of three. This, of course, has a most significant impact on the substance of the original covenantal community: we may no longer speak of an interpersonal commitment alone; rather, the human pair is committed to the third, Divine, partner—much as He is committed to them. Indeed, from the human side, at least, it is this newly defined commitment that defines and legitimates the personal relationship, ensuring that it becomes more than a pact for mutual satisfaction. It is in loyalty to the third party and His charge, that the two find the meaning of their relationship. This reading, needless to say, virtually hangs on a hair. At the same time, it responds in a most sensitive way to God's matchmaking role, if I may borrow a midrashic *motif.* More significantly, perhaps it is thoroughly coherent with the continuation of the narrative, as God will command the pair, and they will sin before Him, thus betraying the commitment in which their community was formed. It is perhaps obvious that all this is a model of Jewish existence, adumbrated in the Genesis narrative.

It would come as no surprise that much of what the Rav does adapts or reworks traditional rabbinic readings, but a discussion of the ways in which this adaptation is worked out is beyond the scope of this essay. I would, however, like to make some brief comment about the relationship of R. Soloveitchik's treatment to certain trends in twentieth-century European Biblical scholarship and thought.

R. Soloveitchik, as we have seen, views the creation of Adam and Eve as embodying a covenantal, dialogic relationship. The influence of Buber cannot be missed; this influence is present in much of the Rav's work, but no more than in "The Lonely Man of Faith." The covenantal idea is, of course, basic to classical Jewish thought, but traditional exegesis does not stress the dialogic character of the foundational relationship of Adam and Eve. Here, then, Buber may have contributed to R. Soloveitchik's reading of Genesis. But it is not only Buber. The dialogic model is fairly commonplace in German exegesis. It is found, as we might expect, in Eichrodt's *Theology of the Old Testament*.[8] It is expounded in massive proportions, however, by Karl Barth. Indeed, the entire forty-first section of the *Church Dogmatics*—a discussion of some three hundred pages—is entitled "Creation and Covenant," where "covenant" has a highly dialogic character.[9]

It is difficult not to perceive the similarity in atmosphere in these works of Barth and R. Soloveitchik; they simply breathe the same conceptual, literary, and hermeneutic air. (R. Soloveitchik read Barth; he comments on him in the notes to the early *Halakhic Man* and *Halakhic Mind*.[10]) This similarity extends, of course, to their treatment of Adam and Eve. Both insist on a dialogic reading of the original human relationship, to be sure. But the parallels go far beyond the assertion of the broad covenantal theme. Barth, for example, also finds significance in man's naming of the natural world, a naming that is in reality an unsuccessful search for companionship. And perhaps less unexpectedly than R. Soloveitchik, Barth focuses on the fact that Adam must be wounded so that Eve can be created. Yet beyond

---

[8] W. Eichrodt, *Theology of the Old Testament*, II (London, 1967), pp. 121, 127, citing previous work.

[9] Karl Barth, *Church Dogmatics*, vol. 3, pt. 1 (Edinburgh, 1958), pp. 176–228 ("Creation as the External Basis of the Covenant") deals with Genesis 1: 24–31, while pp. 228–329 ("The Covenant as the Internal Basis of Creation"), deals with the creation of Adam and Eve in Genesis 2.

[10] See *Halakhic Man*, p. 139, n. 4; *The Halakhic Mind*, New York, 1986, p. 129, n. 93. I am grateful to Prof. Kaplan for pointing out these references to me.

the similarities, manifold differences do exist; and I shall briefly note those that are most significant and characteristic.

R. Soloveitchik, as we have seen, makes a sharp distinction between First Adam and Second Adam, between the person created in Genesis 1 and the person created in Genesis 2. First Adam may be majestic and dignified, but covenantal dialogic existence is bestowed on Second Adam. Barth does not distinguish at all between the two Adam's, as he treats the two narratives as a virtual continuity. This is not merely a difference in literary esthetic alone, however. For Barth, it is precisely this dialogic possibility that forms the "image of God" in man (the motif found in Genesis 1, of course). This dialogic possibility exists then first in God, Who prefaces this very act of creation with the invitation: "Let *us* make man in *our image* . . ." Barth's reading, not unexpectedly, is solidly in the Christological exegetical tradition of Genesis 1:26. Jewish tradition, however, is not committed to any single understanding of the "image of God" in man, which leaves R. Soloveitchik fairly free to cast the net of his imagination, or, alternatively, to exploit this motif for his own purposes. Moreover, as I have suggested, he tends to read materials—even Biblical materials—in a mode that suggests contrasts and distinctions at least as much as continuities,[11] a habit of mind possibly deriving from halakhic studies. In this particular case, he pursues his own agenda, which has a dual focus the celebration and affirmation of technological man, and the painful awareness of the gap between utilitarian fulfillment and true covenantal existence.

There is, I believe, a second and even more interesting difference in the way our materials are handled by Barth and R. Soloveitchik, one that relates directly to the substance of the covenant that is posited by both. For Barth,[12] the covenant between Adam and Eve prefigures the covenant between Israel and God. Now, the relationship of man and woman has, to shift to colloquial usage, its "ups and downs," and here Barth especially stresses the problematics of the erotic component of this relationship. Initially posited in the ideal terms of Genesis 2, it will degenerate in the corruption of sin—especially sexual sin. And so

---

[11] For a broader analysis of the dialectical elements in R. Soloveitchik's thought, see E. Luz, "The Dialectic Element in R. Soloveitchik's Works" (Heb.), *Da'at* 9 (1982), pp. 75–89.

[12] Ibid., p. 312.

the covenant of Israel and the Lord will also know betrayal. But Adam and Eve embody, as well, the ideal covenant—that which inheres not only in the ideal relationship of man and woman or even of Israel and God, but of Jesus and the Church. Now, what is important for our purposes is the theological-literary structure envisioned by Barth. God is not covenanted to Adam and Eve; their covenantal relationship with each other, rather, is a model of His relationship with a corresponding partner—Israel or the Church.

R. Soloveitchik constructs the covenantal reality of God in a totally different way, as we have seen. God, for him, is a covenantal partner *with* Adam and Eve; He is intrinsic to their ideal relationship. On the level of human dynamics, R. Soloveitchik argues that it is the presence of God—a commanding presence that demands mutual commitment to the goals He sets down—which introduces substantive content and value to the human relationship. Yet, by entering into the covenantal relationship, God also commits Himself to the human pair. Both this commitment and the intimacy it implies are adumbrations of God's relationship with His people Israel, a relationship of mutual commitment and passionate intimacy. For R. Soloveitchik, unlike Barth, the relationship of God and people is not symbolically or metaphorically present in the relationship between the first pair; rather, the covenant between these two humans includes God as a third partner.

This distinction can be expressed in a less abstract way as well. It seems that the dialogic relationship expresses itself, for Barth, in the ongoing relationship of two human beings, be it erotic, domestic, and so on. The very reality of living together opens the possibility of dialogue. R. Soloveitchik, however, posits a relationship that is covenantal if it strives towards a normative goal, that is to say an ideal world to which the human pair is dedicated. Dialogue, here, has a halakhic character; the medium itself is *not* the message. Thus it is no surprise—unusual as it may be in the world of Orthodox Judaism—that R. Soloveitchik dedicated "The Lonely Man of Faith" to his wife, describing her in his dedication as "a woman of . . . total commitment and uncompromising truthfulness."

# The Jewish People

## I

It is generally thought, and correctly so, that the individual is at the heart of Rabbi Joseph B. Soloveitchik's thought and writings. The titles of major works tell the story: *Halakhic Man*, "The Lonely Man of Faith." It may be a matter of debate whether the Rav is correctly placed in the existentialist camp, but it cannot be denied that the intellectual, psychological, and spiritual experience of the individual forms the hot core of these and other works. This focus on the person may mark the Rav's halakhic writing as well as his philosophical *oeuvre*. Surely it is no coincidence that major essays, as well as years of classroom teaching, were devoted to *teshuvah*, prayer, and mourning, all topics of individual experience; and that a basic problematic in the Rav's treatment of these topics was the relationship between performance and internalization. Needless to say, the Rav encompassed the entire spectrum of halakhah in his *shiurim* from *Kodashim* to *Nezikin*. But at the same time he seems to have taken a special pleasure in demonstrating that *Berakhot*, say, could sustain the rigor of halakhic discussion no less than did *Bava Metzia*.

This stress should not obscure the fact that the community, and specifically the Jewish community of course, has also been a central concern of the Rav, and that much of his written work focuses on the community as a phenomenological and halakhic entity and grapples with the historical situation of the Jewish people in the modern world. True, the Rav's analysis of the individual provides basic categories through which the community is perceived. More significantly, a basic problematic of R. Soloveitchik's writing is the tension between the individual's personal reality and his role as a member of a community and people. This tension is rendered all the more stubborn by the fact that the Rav relates to peoplehood on a number of different, and indeed shifting, levels. In a sense, though, all this merely underscores the place of peoplehood and community in the Rav's thought, and his commitment to its inescapable centrality.

## II

The tension of individual and community is raised explicitly by the Rav in a number of essays, and in a manner that makes it clear that he is quite aware of the basic modernity of the problematic. Typically, the problem is raised from the point of view of the individual consciousness rather than, say, from the point of view of God or history so we may say that the ultimate conclusion is given at the outset. Be this as it may, the essay appropriately entitled "Community" opens with the question:

> The very instant we pronounce the word "community" we recall, by sheer association, the ancient controversy between collectivism and individualism. Willy nilly the old problem of who and what comes first (metaphysically, not chronologically) arises. Is the individual an independent free entity, who gives up basic aspects of his sovereignty in order to live within a communal framework; or is the reverse true: the individual is born into the community, which, in turn, invests him with certain rights? This perennial controversy is still unresolved.[1]

In this particular treatment, the Rav asserts that no clear-cut choice is possible-though once again the answer itself is formulated from the perspective of the individual consciousness and experience.

And let us give a simple answer; Judaism rejects both alternatives; neither theory, *per se,* is true. Both experiences, that of aloneness, as well as that of togetherness, are inseparable basic elements of the I-awareness.[2]

---

[1] Joseph B. Soloveitchik, "Community," *Tradition* XVII, 2 (Spring, 1978), p. 7. Available at www.traditiononline.org.

[2] Ibid.

Characteristically, the community itself is no faceless collective but rather a network of individual relationships—a description that becomes significant as the essay unfolds.

If no clear-cut resolution is possible or desirable in "Community," a decisive set of priorities is articulated in other discussions. The homily entitled "God or People—Which Comes First?" is in fact a discussion of our issue, for "God" = individual spirituality.[3] God, of course, will come first. Here the Rav uses a traditional midrash with striking effect, as he builds on the midrashic priority *of parah adumah* (the Red Heifer) over *korban Pesah* (the Paschal Sacrifice). The Paschal sacrifice symbolizes the national component of Judaism, while the Red Heifer bestows personal purity—and it is the latter that is the more significant.

It is quite apparent that the different resolutions of the tension in these essays reflect, in fact, different aspects of the experience of peoplehood. The priority of God (or individual spiritual experience) over peoplehood expresses the relative insignificance of the people as a political, nationalistic collective. Against this reality, the individual is of far greater significance. This evaluation is revised however when one considers the people not as *collective* but as *community*. As community, the people remain in dialectical equipoise with the individual, and little conflict is felt.

---

[3] "Which Comes First, God or People?" in Abraham Besdin, ed., *Reflections of the Rav* (Jerusalem 1979), 107–16. A similar evaluation of the relative weight of individual and community emerges from the following, mildly ambiguous passage:

> Moreover, the halakhah's concern with man is mainly centered on the individual. Man is neither an idea, like humanity, whose praise Plato and the Greek philosophers sang, nor a supra-individual unity, like society or community, which many philosophical systems, including that of Marxism, have idealized and idolized. They sang the praise of society, which is supra-individual unity. The halakhah insists that nothing, not the idea nor the collective, should supplant the single transient and frail individual "who is here today and tomorrow is in the grave" (Berakhot 28b), who today is here on the platform, and the next day, who knows where he will end up. He occupies a dominant position in the halakhah, and his role is central and indispensable. Of course, the halakhah has not overlooked the community, particularly the community of the committed and the elected, as the barrier to the Divine eternal message. Yet, the individual constitutes a reality whose ontic legitimacy must not be questioned and whose interest the halakhah, like a devoted mother, has at heart. ("A Halakhic Approach to Suffering," in Joseph B. Soloveitchik, *Out of the Whirlwind*, eds. David Shatz, Joel B. Wolowelsky, and Reuven Ziegler (Meotzar Harav/KTAV, Jersey City, 2003), pp. 94–95.

The pattern just outlined provides the basic grid for the Rav's discussion of the Two Adams in "The Lonely Man of Faith." Here too the assertion is made that man is a member of two communities. The prime focus in this essay is, of course, the individual, or more precisely, the type. But discussion of the Two Adams quickly develops into discussion of the different communities produced by these different human types. The Rav cannot discuss Adam without relating him simultaneously to the community he forms: man cannot be understood only as individual. First Adam, we recall, represents majestic, technological Man. Never in search of Eve—as Man and Woman appear simultaneously in the first account of creation in Genesis—First Adam is ontologically complete. The formation of a collective by First Adam (and his coupling with Eve?) is a natural act, rationalized by Social Contract ideology and serving functional need. This collective is, of course, a political entity. Second Adam, on the other hand, appears alone; and his search for Eve is driven by the recognition that loneliness is fundamental to his being. By his commitment in faith to Eve he forms the first covenantal community, a community in which God the Creator is a third partner. This community bears an ontological character and is the pattern for the covenantal faith community of Israel.

"The Lonely Man of Faith" is, of course, devoted to the dialectical relationship of the Two Adams, and asserts the fundamental integrity of each as rooted in the biblical presentation of Man. Technological Man is not merely an instrumental creature in the service of Covenantal Man, but is rather recognized as a unique expression of human striving and fulfillment of a divine command encoded in humanity. Technological man is not to be transcended or conquered; his world-developing activity remains an eternal embodiment of the biblical imperative. In drawing this image of "majestic" First Adam, R. Soloveitchik enthusiastically endows Western scientific technology with the fullest acknowledgment Judaism could offer. And since technological man is also collective man, the acknowledgment extended to First Adam embraces his latter manifestation as well, though it is clear that R. Soloveitchik is much more entranced by humanity's scientific abilities than by its political bent.

R. Soloveitchik does indeed allow man's technological ability a significant role in the Divine scheme; "majestic" First Adam realized his potential and fulfills a godly mandate by subduing the physical world and perfecting it. But the positive appropriation of this major characteristic of Western civilization is not accompanied by a corresponding imperative to appropriate Western culture, its philosophical or literary achievements. This assertion seems improbable, or at least paradoxical, with regard to the Rav, whose major writings are suffused with modern Western philosophy and literature, and whose very intellectual world is constructed, in part at least, with materials provided by modern culture. Yet the paradox is fact; the Rav is a paradigm of the synthesis of Jewish and Western culture, but he nowhere *prescribes* this move or even urges its legitimacy. Are we to assume, then, that this silence discloses a measure of ambivalence, as though the Rav is hinting that he cannot fully approve of involvement in Western culture, or even that there is no systematic way to make it part of the spiritual curriculum?

My own feeling is that quite the opposite happened. Technology is, after all, concrete and materialistic; it raises the standard of living but does not necessarily enhance our spiritual or even human quality of life—nor is that its intention. Technology, then, needs rabbinic approval and even defense. This is of course not true of philosophy, literature, music. These, despite their potential dangers, are intrinsically related to the noetic and spiritual component of human existence. It is obvious that they should be cultivated and that the Jew who strives for a fuller spiritual existence will be open to their message and impact. The Rav's silence would derive, then, from the very example he provides. How, after reading *Ish ha-Halakhah,* could one imagine that Max Scheler and William James are not required reading? Indeed, that they will not contribute to one's spiritual formation?

But despite the enduring dialectic relationship of First and Second Adam, the assertion that neither can or should strive to subdue the other, it is Second Adam who has axiological priority, and the values he embodies that rank the higher. Second Adam, united in covenantal relation with Eve, adumbrates the covenantal community of Israel, which enters a covenantal relationship with God; such community obviously ranks higher than the political collective of First Adam. And—

as is implied in "Community"—the human individual, self-conscious and ontologically lonely and searching, will also be seen as more value-laden than the political-technological collective. For spiritual, ethical existence is to be created only within the reality of the community and the being of the person; it is not an aspect of the functional collective.

The fundamental issue for the Rav will be the relationship of this person with this community. R. Soloveitchik often returns to the assertion that the Jewish community is a metaphysical entity:

> The community in Judaism is not a functional-utilitarian, but an ontological one. The community is not just an assembly of people who work together for their mutual benefit, but a metaphysical entity, an individuality; I might say, a living whole. In particular, Judaism has stressed the wholeness and the unity of *Knesset Israel*, the Jewish community. The latter is not a conglomerate. It is an autonomous entity, endowed with a life of its own. We, for instance, lay claim to *Eretz Israel*. God granted the land to us as a gift. To whom did He pledge the land? Neither to an individual, nor to a partnership consisting of millions of people. He gave it to the *Knesset Israel*, to the community as an independent unity, as a distinct juridic metaphysical person. He did not promise the land to me, to you, to them; nor did He promise the land to all of us together. Abraham did not receive the land as an individual, but as the father of a future nation. The owner of the Promised Land is the *Knesset Israel*, which is a community persona.[4]

In halakhic terms—and the halakhic plane provides a highly significant legitimation for any Jewish idea—community is *tzibbur*, rather than *shuttafut* (partnership), which in its functional overtones suggests the collective. Major halakhic phenomena are interpreted in terms of the overarching integrity of the community: the *viddui* (confession) and sounding of the *shofar* on the Days of Awe are structured, in part, as communal acts: the efficacy of the Scapegoat and the very

---

[4] "Community," p. 9.

forgiveness on *Yom Kippur are* mediated to the individual through his organic participation (in the dual sense of activity and grounding) in the community;[5] worship too has its communal expression in the prayer of the *sheliah tzibbur,* which is not only a functional repetition of the individual's prayer, but a fundamentally novel and independent ritual act.[6] In all this, the Rav draws upon both ancient and modern thought: midrashic-kabbalistic notions of *Knesset Israel* as well as Hegelian and Romantic concepts of the spiritual uniqueness of peoples. And, as we shall see, the halakhic and conceptual analysis will be supplemented by a deeply emotional stress.

The very examples just cited make the point. However spiritual the Jewish person is as individual, the forms of his spirituality are given him by his rootedness in *Knesset Israel.* More radically, his full relationship with God is mediated through this community-people, for God's promise and commitment is to no individual but only to His people. The people, a metaphysical entity, is possessed of undoubted existence and continuity and able to enter a relationship with God. The individual is lost without this bestowal; totally alone, he cannot take flight to the Alone, who in a sense, is also not totally alone.

And yet, despite the fact that this community transcends the person and bestows upon him the forms of spiritual life and the possibility of God's forgiveness and acceptance, the matter is surprisingly not so simple or one-sided. For the community is constituted by virtue of the ontological loneliness of the individual, as we have seen; this may not be any more of a historical statement than is Rousseau's Social Contract, but it does describe the essential phenomenon. Immediately after describing *Knesset Israel* as a "metaphysical entity," the Rav asserts that "the personalistic unity and reality of a community, such as *Knesset Israel,* is due to the philosophy of existential complementarity of the individuals belonging to the *Knesset Israel.*"[7] It may be, of course, that this latter enlargement upon and modernizing interpretation of Halevi's much more modest analysis of the praying community, ought to

---

[5] *On Repentance,* pp. 109–37.

[6] *Shiurim le-Zekher Abba Mari, z"l,* II (Jerusalem, 1985), pp. 17–34.

[7] "Community," pp. 9–10. For elaboration of this idea in kabbalistic terms, see *Yemei Zikkaron* (Jerusalem, 1986), pp. 59–62.

be seen in the context of the social workers' conference in which it was made—yet one also ought not to make too much of this fact.

This rather strange situation finds consistent expression in the fact that the community itself is often valorized through experiences that are primarily personal. The political component of communal existence is not highlighted, as we have seen, and when the Rav does focus on the national-historical aspect of Jewish existence (a theme to which we turn shortly), he frequently elaborates on the motif of Jewry's "loneliness" as a people, a motif that owes as much to his understanding of personal life as it does to Numbers 22:9. The individual himself, we hear, is ideally part of his community not by virtue of biology or citizenship, but rather through his appropriation of the community's values—and these values are those concretized in personal spiritual achievement. The following sequence, in which relationship to the organic historical community is in fact mediated through a primarily personal commitment (Torah), is typical:

> The Jew who believes in *Knesset Israel* is the Jew who lives as part of it wherever it is and is willing to give his life for it, feels its pain, rejoices with it, fights in its wars, groans at its defeats and celebrates its victories. The Jew who believes in *Knesset Israel* is a Jew who binds himself with inseverable bonds not only to the People of Israel of his own generation but to the community of Israel throughout the ages. How so? Through the Torah which embodies the spirit and the destiny of Israel from generation to generation unto eternity.[8]

The pains and joys, victories and defeats, all the experiences that accompany normal historical-national existence, very much demand the Jew's identification. Ultimately, though, these experiences seem rooted in temporality, in "the Jewish people of this generation." "*Knesset Israel* of all generations" is joined only through Torah.[9] It is a "prayerful,

---

[8] *On Repentance*, p.137.

[9] See *Perakim*, pp. 84–85. Cf. *Beit ha-Levi* (by the Rav's great-grandfather), Homily XVIII, printed as an appendix to *Responsa Beit ha-Levi*, II (Warsaw, 1874). Comparison of this and other aspects of the Rav's essays with these homilies is beyond the scope of this essay. In gen-

charitable, teaching community, which feels the breath of eternity"—
so the concluding sentence of "Community." Certainly, it is not insignificant that two of the three characteristics listed—praying and teaching—are primarily personal acts.

## III

"Kol Dodi Dofek" is universally read as the Rav's major statement on
Jewish peoplehood. In Israel, I believe, it is often taught as a Zionist
statement. Its Zionism, of course, is a very diasporic Zionism:
American Jews are asked to provide money and political support,
not *aliyah*;[10] and even support for Israel frequently shades into support
for *yeshivot*.[11] On the other hand, "Kol Dodi Dofek"—and one cannot overlook the history of Messianic interpretation given this verse
in Song of Songs—asserts the providential quality of the State's birth,
making its historical emergence an act of divine intervention. It is impossible, then, not to identify with the existence of the State, and R.
Soloveitchik does so full-throatedly and whole-heartedly. This act of
identification, frequently reasserted, ought not to be underestimated.[12]
The Rav has described quite frankly the emotional and social price he
paid for his Zionism. The family tradition of Brisk, he reminds us, was

---

eral, the homilies of *Beit ha-Levi* also ought to be read in the light of the 19th-century haskalah
and other social developments in the Jewish community.

[10] But see Arnold Eisen. *Galut* (Indiana U. Press, 1986), p. 166.

[11] Indeed, the Rav occasionally seems discomfited by the halakhic value of certain physical
aspects of Israel's involvement with its land. Thus, in interpreting the rabbinic assertion that
the land's holiness was established more permanently by *hazakah* (possession) then by *kibbush* (conquest), the Rav understands *hazakah* in two distinct ways—neither, though, elaborates the meaning of physical occupation. See P. H. Peli (ed.), *On Repentance*, pp. 330–39
(*U-Vikkashtem mi-Sham, in Ish ha-Halakhah—Galui ve-Nistar* [Jerusalem, 1979], p. 191,
n. 17) and *Hamesh Derashot* (Jerusalem, 1974) pp. 42–44 (Naturally, I am aware that this
is, in a sense, an argument from silence and that it makes ideological capital from halakhic
*hiddush*. Nonetheless—*devarim be-go*?) Note the parallel spiritualizing moment in the Rav's
assertion that "holiness" of Ramban and Yehuda HaLevi was no greater in the Land of Israel
than in *galut*: "Personally, emotionally, I simply cannot accept the fact of the diminished
holiness of these masters while in *galut*. . . . For in a spiritual sense, they never were in *galut*"
(*Hamesh Derashot*, p. 93).

[12] See also Michael Rosenak, "Ha-Adam ha-Yehudi ve-ha-Medina," in S. Israeli, ed., *Sefer
ha-Yovel li-Khevod ha-Rav Yosef Soloveitchik* (Jerusalem, 1984), I, 152–53, on the significant
impact of the Rav's religious-zionist affiliation and involvement.

quite anti-Zionist—and one need not belabor the Rav's intense attachment to the traditions of his family. Here the Biblical Joseph[13] serves as a powerfully moving paradigm, for he too knew the pain of separation from his brethren, the price knowingly paid for his people's survival in a new and necessary reality:

> I was not born into a Zionist household . . . If I now identify with the Mizrachi, against my family tradition, it is only because . . . I feel that Divine Providence ruled like "Joseph" and against his brothers . . . I built an altar. . . . The altar still stands today, with smoke rising from the sacrifice upon it . . . [14]

Actually, though, the Zionism of "Kol Dodi Dofek" is not really its most interesting aspect, though it may dominate most of the essay. Much more interesting, to my mind, is the way the Rav comes to grips with the nature and reality of Jewish peoplehood in the twentieth century, and more specifically, in the generation *of Sho'ah* (and Statehood). Once accepted as reality, it is assimilated into aggadic and philosophic typology, and becomes part of the paradigmatic reality of Torah. The typology that emerges has substantial roots in classical, premodern, Jewish thought, but it is nonetheless shaped as a response to a distinctly modern situation and reflects, in part, the modern experience and even value of Jewish peoplehood.

The reality of Jewish peoplehood in the twentieth century is, of course, a largely secular reality. The Jewish people have become a people of nonbelievers in any traditional halakhic measure. All that is really left is belief in the people itself, whether in its American or Israeli version, belief in national existence in history. This, I think, is the reality the Rav sees. One traditional option is to turn away, inward, acknowledging as

---

[13] R. Soloveitchik frequently returns to the figure of Joseph in his *derashot*. A discussion of this theme is beyond the scope of this essay; I would simply point out that the Joseph material, which often focuses on either cultural pluralism or familial separation and reconciliation (often interweaving both these themes) is especially poignant.

[14] *Five Addresses*, pp. 34–36. Actually, the move towards Religious-Zionism had already been made, and the sacrifice brought, by R. Moshe Soloveitchik, the Rav's father. Nonetheless, the integrity of the anti-Zionist position possessed its attractions, as *"Ma Dodekh mi-Dod,"* the Rav's eulogy of his uncle, indicates. See Eisen, *op. cit.*, p. 169.

"true Jews" only the remaining adherents to traditional behavior and belief. This option is usually complemented by the assertion that, of course, all children of Jewish parents (mothers, that is) remain halakhically Jewish. The Rav does adopt this option—in part. But he goes far beyond it in that he develops a model for identification with this secular Jewish reality, even as he asserts that it must be transcended.

Two models of Jewish existence are posited: Jews of fate, and Jews of destiny and purpose. The first reflects Jewishness as biological fact, as national identity into which the Jew is born. The second reflects Jewishness as chosen commitment to spirituality and *mitzvot*. The first model displays the Jew as passive; the second as active. The Jew of fate is largely defined by the historical role imposed on the people Israel as objects of persecution; the Jew of destiny defines his own spiritual identity as creator of culture transcending physical survival. The Rav realizes, of course, that even physical survival in the context of Jewish fate requires immense energy and organization, so that the "active-passive" distinction does not function as an empirical description. The point, rather, is whether the Jew is responding to the initiatives taken by others as they attempt to impose their vision of the Jews' place upon him, or whether he chooses his own identity. In terms familiar to the student of modern European thought, we may speak of the Jew as object of the will of others or as subject of his own will.[15] And in terms of modern Jewish thought, the distinction reminds one of the Zionist critique of passive diaspora existence as against the self-determining political activity demanded of the Jew. For the Rav, the Jew of destiny and purpose is characterized as the Jew who chooses his halakhic-covenantal identity, though, of course, this identity may also require historical, even political, behavior. These paradigms focus motifs familiar in other works of the Rav: we hear echoes of the distinction between collective and community that has already occupied us (thus the Rav also distinguishes *mahaneh* and *edah*), and the distinction along the active-passive axis reminds us of creative Halakhic Man, though both First and Second Adam are also creative individuals (though in very different ways).

---

[15] These categories figure prominently in the analysis of a self-creation in *Halakhic Man*.

No less significant than the paradigmatic terminology, however, are the biblical models for this typology, models that clearly embody modern concerns.

The Jew of fate is symbolized by Egyptian bondage; the Jew of destiny and purpose, by the Torah received at Sinai. Egyptian slavery, the symbolic embodiment of Jewish historical fate, is a patent symbol of Holocaust, much as the deliverance from that bondage is a patent symbol of the rebirth of national political existence in the State of Israel. Slavery and Exodus precede Sinai, and in the Rav's presentation, are experiences of a people that has not (yet) reached Sinai. Slavery and redemption are, then, in this homily on biblical history, the experience of secular Jews—yet these experiences are inalienable elements of Jewish identity. This move is clearly shaped by the reality of the Holocaust; this happened to secular Jews, and this is paradigmatic of classic Jewish existence. The inability to deny these facts leads to an acceptance of the purely national aspect of Jewish existence as rooted in biblical models and as objects of Jewish identification.

Obviously, all this has ancient halakhic and aggadic roots. A Jew remains a Jew, halakhically, whatever his behavior or beliefs. And the aggadah discusses the "sonship" to God of wicked and even defecting Jews. In much later times, one can point to the idea of the *pintele Yid* that remains, inextinguishable, in every born Jew, an idea stressed by both the *Tanya* and *Nefesh ha-Hayyim*. Of special interest in this context is Homily XVI of *Beit ha-Levi*, which develops the distinction between *ani ha-Shem* and *benei ha-Shem* as parallel to pious and impious Jews, with even the latter remaining *benei ha-Shem*.[16] The Rav goes beyond this, however, in one significant sense. These earlier discussions relate, fundamentally, to the Jew *qua* individual and his status. But the discussion in "Kol Dodi Dofek" is devoted to the Jewish *people*: collective and community bear the fate and destiny of Jewry, and the biblical models explored are models of historical, national experience. All this clearly points to the fact that the Rav is interested in contemporary historical reality, which is not a

---

[16] The distinction, along with appropriate terminology, is of course much older; see, e.g., Ramban to Exodus 14:10. But similar ideas also figured in modern Jewish thought: see Nathan Rotenstreich, *Ha-Mahshavah ha-Yehudit baEt ha-Hadashah*, 1, pp. 166ff, on Buber's distinction between *am* and *umah* and on its roots in modern European thought.

matter of individual behavior but rather a pattern encompassing an entire people; not a question of an individual's status (or providential recompense) but rather of what the nation endures in history. R. Soloveitchik returns repeatedly in his *derashot* to the fact that the Nazis persecuted all Jews equally, irrespective of their religious commitment or lack of same. The *pintele Yid* motif seemingly reflects the eternal focus on the Jew as victim, rather than the ineradicable spiritual imprinting to which he is supposedly heir. It is almost as though the moving force behind "Kol Dodi Dofek," then, is the Holocaust and only secondarily the declaration of the State of Israel. Both these experiences, symbolized by different but related aspects of the Egyptian bondage, focus on the classically Jewish fate of secular Jews and their community. The Rav would not close his eyes to this reality, and so he transmuted it through homiletic typology into Jewish doctrine.

Jewish identity is not defined exclusively by Sinai and Torah—it also includes Egypt and its Jews. Nor is Jewish loyalty directed exclusively to the community of Sinai, as it too is broad enough to include the Jews of Egypt. The Rav frequently stressed (in both oral presentations and in his writings) that a Jew dare not alienate himself from his people. There is a classic halakhic base to all this, of course, inasmuch as a Jew always remains such, but this norm is now filled with historical and especially *emotional* contents—all this in the crucible of the modern Jewish experience. The Rav would often cite Maimonides' ruling that even the Jew who is not guilty of any sin—the "observant" Jew—may lose his share in eternal life if he alienates himself from the community and does not willingly share its historical travail.[17] For the Rav, Maimonides speaks not only of concrete dissociation from actual Jewish fate, but even of the alienated consciousness.

There is a sense, then, in which the realization that the Jewish people exists as a secular reality (with a sacred charge and potential, of course) is reflected in the content and quality of Jewish loyalty. The Rav will be openly critical of observant Jews ("Jews of destiny and purpose") who are unable to embrace secular Jews ("Jews of fate") as organic parts of their

---

[17] *Hilkhot Teshuvah* 3:6.

commitment to *Knesset Israel*.[18] This attitude dovetails with an intense relationship with the entirety of Jewish history. On the whole, it is true, the significant moments of Jewish history are evoked by Abayye and Rava, Rashi and Rabbenu Tam, the Gaon of Vilna and the *Ba'al ha-Tanya,* that is, by moments of spiritual-intellectual achievement. But other modes of identification operate, too. The Rav analyzes incisively the rather tepid response of religious Jewry to the State of Israel and more specifically to the idea of *akvah,* as an indication that this Jewry grasps the Land of Israel in normative halakhic terms alone, rather than by participation in "the yearnings of past generations."[19] Such emotional yearning grows from an identification with the totality of Jewish life and the totality of Jewish society. Naturally, this society was a traditional society, and its "yearnings" were pervaded by traditional values and expressed in traditional terms. Yet this focus on historical solidarity remains significant.[20]

Clearly, then, "Kol Dodi Dofek" grapples with the secular reality of Jewish peoplehood, and it may even reflect the growing significance of the idea of peoplehood in modern Jewish thought and life. At the same time, its typology sets limits. Whereas First Adam and Second Adam exist in dialectic tandem, with only a hint of the axiological priority of the latter, Egypt and Sinai, the Jew of fate and the Jew of destiny and purpose clearly reflect a hierarchical order. Sinai will build on Egypt, and Jewish historical fate is a permanent feature of Jewish existence, but precious little in the way of Jewish values will emerge from the victimized identity of bondage. Even Redemption, so charged an experience in Jewish thought and experience, occurs to a passive people and does not bear the message of self-transcendence.

---

[18] *Five Addresses*, pp. 147–48.

[19] *Be-Sod ha-Yahid ve-ha-Yahad*, pp. 417–18.

[20] See David Hartman's account of Rabbi Soloveitchik's charge to students as he ordained them to be rabbis:

"I have entrusted to you the spiritual message and treasure of the Jewish people throughout history. Halakhah says that if one harms a person, one must ask for forgiveness. And if the person in question has died, halakhah demands that one goes to the cemetery, that one finds his grave and that one publicly declares one's guilt and begs for forgiveness. Now—I want you to remember one thing always: we do not know where all the graves of more than three thousand years of Jewish history are. I entrust to you the heritage of the people of Israel. (David Hartman, *Joy and Responsibility* [Jerusalem], p. 223)."

"Kol Dodi Dofek" itself does not, of course, develop this tension. On the contrary, its basic thrust lies in the welding of these disparate Jewish experiences into one emotional whole. Indeed R. Soloveitchik tells us of the values that emerge in a people that must struggle to ensure its physical survival; mutuality, sympathy, self-sacrifice, *hesed*. These are the functional values of the collective to be sure, but they also require the individual to transcend his own selfish concerns and, as *hesed* (the term used in this context by the Rav), resonate deeply in the Jewish consciousness. The Rav also develops the religious symbolism of the "covenant of destiny" and ensures its permanent place in the spiritual totality of Jewish experience. The two ritual acts in conversion—circumcision and immersion—reflect the two covenants that are thus integral factors in Jewish identity. Circumcision symbolizes that which is carved painfully into the historic body of the Jewish people; elsewhere, indeed, no less a figure than father Abraham, first of all Jews to be circumcised and founder of the Jewish people as family, is presented as the forebear of the Covenant of Fate. Immersion, the Rav continues, symbolizes the active spiritual moment in which the potential Jew chooses a life in community, with God.[21] Yet despite this positive appropriation of the Covenant of Fate and of the historic fact of Jewish peoplehood, there is also a deep ambivalence, or better, unease, which is only hinted at by these two disparate symbols of Egypt and Sinai.

Despite R. Soloveitchik's assertion that the national (and in our reading, secular) component of Jewry is an organic part of the Jewish people, for it too suffers the historical fate of Jewry (as in Egypt), it is also not uncommon for him to slip into a different literary mode, and both mood and content change. This is best exemplified by his "political sermons," the *derashot* delivered at annual Mizrachi conventions and published as *Hamesh Derashot*. Delivered to religious American Zionists, these talks were really directed at the Religious-Zionist leadership in Israel, with the American audience serving, apparently, as pretext. The policy issue discussed in these talks is: How ought the Religious-Zionist party relate to

---

[21] *Fate and Destiny*, pp. 60–63. See also *On Repentance*, pp. 234–38; here, too, Abraham and the *avot* in general signify the inescapable element in Jewish fate, as does circumcision, while *kabbalat mitzvot* (the convert's acceptance of *mitzvot*), ratner than *tevilah*, symbolizes the freely chosen moment of integration with Jewish destiny. See also n. 24.

the secular government? What is particularly interesting in our context is not the substantive answer presented by the Rav, who advises a rather aggressive stance, but rather its literary vehicle. In *derashah* after *derashah* secular Israeli leadership is midrashically assimilated to the non-Jewish biblical oppressor: Esau, Pharaoh, Avimelekh, Abraham's servant-lads, Amon and Moab. This, of course, is no more than literary and perhaps routine symbolism, yet it ought not to be dismissed out of hand, for it discloses a basic level of consciousness. The secular Jew has ceased being a real Jew, though he too will eventually return. Perhaps, though, it were wise to remember that R. Soloveitchik's hostility is directed at the leadership of an opposing ideology, and that it is evoked in a political context that always stimulates the polemical.[22]

Nonetheless, this literary symptom ought to be pursued more deeply. It would be helpful. I think, to put the matter in terms familiar from the ideology developed by Rabbi A. I. Kook. Rav Kook, needless to say, is also capable of using similar symbols for similar homiletical purposes. But his main thrust moves in quite a different direction. Now, it is likely that the contrast between the Rav and R. Kook reflects different metaphysical orientations no less than differing attitudes towards modern Jewish nationalism and towards halakhah. I will be concerned nonetheless with the contrast as it appears on the ideological, rather than on the metaphysical, level.

R. Soloveitchik does not seem to think that classical Judaism, as it is presently understood, suffers from any basic flaw. It—as distinct from the Jewish people—displays no moral or religious malaise. Nor is Jewish history, for that matter, a tale of the ups and downs of Judaism that, given at Sinai, has always retained its fundamental divine strength. halakhah, too, is adequate both in method and substance to its task. Though the Rav will concede that the analytical method of Brisk cast some much-needed light in a darkening room, it is significant that the reform in question was intellectual rather than moral or religious.

---

[22] *Five Addresses*, 109–11, 156–57, 183–84; see Rosenak, *op. cit.*, p. 153, and Risen, *op. cit.*, pp. 167–68. A second major theme of these talks generally is that Mizrachi—rather than the anti-Zionist entities—represents authentic Judaism, and this claim will be further buttressed by attacks on the secular Zionist leadership. Interestingly, these talks betray no illusions as to the likelihood that their audience could be proselytized into *aliyah*; it is clear throughout that American Jews and Israeli Jews were and will continue to be two distinct populations.

Perhaps, too, certain forms of Hasidism added relevant spiritual moments—but nothing more. Certainly, the Rav does not indicate that a renaissance of Judaism is an urgent need. Hence, whatever growth ought to occur will come out of the healthy organic stock of Jewish life and thought, from people who are loyal to halakhah; its values and patterns. Perhaps the most significant challenge of the Orthodox intellectual (and spiritual?) achievement offered by Rabbi Soloveitchik (aside from the political critique in *Hamesh Derashot*) is that which is silently implied by the body of his writing itself: Why did no one else do anything like this work?

Rabbi Soloveitchik, consequently, finds no legitimacy, spiritual grandeur, or subterranean power in antinomian movements or individuals. The move to secularism is not seen as an idealistic rebellion against the inadequacies of the tradition, or an inevitable attempt to reach for moral and religious realities outside the grasp of Torah as currently understood or as potentially understandable by its loyal students. He will not entertain a dialectic according to which religious (and moral?) antinomianism can be admired as a courageous attempt to scale truths unattainable within the context of normal halakhic method and life. The norms of the Torah need not be rejected so that higher spiritual norms may be disclosed or concretized, or even so that historical degeneration may be corrected. Halakhah is to be plumbed, not transcended.

Since no substantive renaissance of Judaism is necessary, the function of a political-national rejuvenation is not to provide such. Zionism is not, in the broadest sense even, a spiritual movement; and if its history includes religious and moral excesses, these have no dialectical justification as the necessary price to be paid for the march to higher spirituality (whether or not that goal is in itself an adequate justification). If Messianism exists in R. Soloveitchik's vocabulary, it is an austerely Maimonidean messianism in which a national-political revival provides a physical base but no intrinsic spiritual content. Zionist leadership will be admired, perhaps even profusely praised, for its achievement in building a physical and social haven. Indeed, the Land of Israel itself is placed on the axis of the Abrahamic covenant of fate.[23] R. Soloveitchik does, I think, go a bit further: I recall his developing the theme that the holiness of the Land was not "mythological" but a function of its providing the context for a holy society—again, a fundamentally Maimonidean orientation. The application of Torah norms to an entire society made, then, for a richer and truer concretization of Torah, for a fuller embodiment of the Jew's fundamental task—but even this is no radical renaissance. This image of the State of Israel as a potential embodiment of the broadest ethical and societal vocation of Judaism, a vocation based on a broad covenantal commitment, is perceived by many students of the Rav to be implicit in his teaching.

Curiously (and regrettably?) this positive and challenging image does not recur frequently in the published texts available to us.[24] For the most part, then, the establishment of the State of Israel is a moment in the battle for physical survival and a significant achievement in the ongoing struggle to create a focus of Jewish identity for Jewries that have lost their traditional moorings in the modern world. And, hopefully, this moment of redemption from the victimizations of Jewish fate (though the State fully shares in the "loneliness" intrinsic to that fate) will lead to a fuller flowering of Jewish purpose. But if ever forced to choose between a secular state of Israel and the God of Israel, "then it must be clearly understood that all of us, with one voice, will choose the God of Israel."[25]

## IV

I have already noted that the significance of community manifests itself no less on the halakhic plane than on the aggadic. This state of affairs is

---

[23] *Five Addresses*, pp. 142–43. It is to be recalled of course, that this Abrahamic community is no mere nationalistic collective but a metaphysical *tzibbur* to which the land has been granted; see at n. 5.

[24] See Rosenak, op. cit.; the survey in A. Ravitzky. "Ha-Kol Tzafui . . .," in A. Hareven, ed., *Yisrael Likrat ha-Me'ah ha-Esrim ve-ha-Ehad* (Jerusalem, 1985), pp. 185–91, with the careful summary at p. 191; Aharon Lichtenstein, "Introduction," in Joseph Epstein, ed., *Shiurei ha-Rav* (New York, 1975), p. 4.

[25] *Five Addresses*, p. 117; Rosenak, p. 166 and n. 36.

symptomatic of the Rav's fundamental orientation to Torah as a whole, for he often asserts that the halakhic sphere is the most significant indicator of authenticity; indeed, this is a major burden of *Halakhic Man*. Now, the priority generally attached to the halakhic over the aggadic itself reflects the central role of community. For halakhah is normative, obliging all members of the community equally, and frequently structured so as to involve them all together,[26] as against the often individualistic, idiosyncratic, and moderately nonnormative quality of aggadah. Put another way: the language of halakhah, its basic forms, are often communal.

The communal aspect of halakhah is of course expressed in specific ways, some of which were noted earlier: prayer, sacrifice, the *shofar*, and confession of the Days of Awe. But R. Soloveitchik devotes considerable attention to another, more general, role of the community within the halakhic scheme—the *community as source of authority*. These discussions are solidly rooted in classical halakhic sources, yet seem at the same time to disclose a modern sensibility. Interestingly, some of the motifs and concerns we have detected in the Rav's evaluation of modern Jewish reality function in his halakhic treatment as well.

It is clear from numerous rabbinic instances that the people Israel function as a legal entity in a variety of spheres, religious as well as civil. As such, halakhah assumes that the people can express its will, so as to confirm or veto rabbinic legislation, for example. Maimonides, by systematizing the process of rabbinic legislation in *Mishneh Torah,* may have further highlighted this phenomenon; he also claimed that one of the bases of Talmudic authority as a whole is the consent of the people Israel. R. Soloveitchik takes Maimonides one step further: popular consent is given an institutional concretization—the Great Sanhedrin.[27]

---

[26] *Halakhic Man*, pp. 42–43.

[27] The following discussion is based on two essays dealing with the calendar and other problems: *Kovetz Hiddushei Torah* (Jerusalem, n.d.) pp. 47–65 and *Shiurim le Zekher Abba Mari,* I (Jerusalem, 1983), pp. 129–34. The latter treatment is apparently a reworking of the former. It is not unlikely that the stress on the representative function of authoritative institutions and on the role of consensual elements reflects modern thinking. But see, too, *Hiddushei R. Yitzhak Ze'ev ha-Levi* (Jerusalem, 1971) to *Hilkhot Sanhedrin* 5:1 (as Prof. Abie Feintuch pointed out to me—or is even R. Velvel a child of modernity. For the role of these notions in classic halakhic materials see my "Individual and Community in the Middle Ages," in D. Elazar, ed., *Kinship and Consent* (Ramat Gan, 1983), pp. 217–59: *Ekronot Mediniyyim be-Mishnat ha*

The Sanhedrin is thus understood as having a dual function, for it expresses the will of the people Israel as well as pronouncing opinions and decisions in its role as the major organ of Oral Law. Thus the Rav points to the interchanging phrases "consent of the majority of Israel" and "consent of the High Court" in Maimonides' definition of national conquest (*kibbush rabbim*). This analysis apparently broadens the scope of rabbinic authority, for the Sanhedrin now speaks for the people as well as for the Torah. Yet a study of the broader context in which this analysis figures indicates a more complex situation. If the Sanhedrin speaks for the people, it is no less clear that its authority, in certain spheres at least, is derived from the people.

This discussion of *kibbush rabbim* is actually a springboard for a much more extended treatment of the principles of authority constituting the Jewish calendrical year. Ideally, according to Maimonides, calendrical decisions are to be taken by an ordained court, a subcommittee as it were of the Great Court. This ideal construct encounters difficulties, obviously, in current (and Maimonidean) historical reality; the Great Court and ordination no longer exist, and yet the calendar does continue to function authoritatively. This is not the place to rehearse in detail the various Maimonidean texts relevant to the problem, of course. The Rav finds a solution in the idea, supported by these texts, that what is really crucial are the calculations done by *benei Eretz Yisrael* ("the Jews of the land of Israel"), or in a later version, the practice of Jewry as a whole.[28] In normal circumstances, of course, the Great Court would itself have the calculations done and issue the proper directives. Yet the fact that this can also be accomplished by "the Jews of the Land of Israel" indicates that the Great Court is in fact the representative of this Jewry, speaks for it, and actually derives its authority (in this and similar administrative matters) from it. As I have pointed out, R. Soloveitchik (in one treatment of this problem, at least) vests the authority of the calendar, ultimately, in the practice of the entire Jewish people, in the holiday celebrations of the entire Jewish people that legitimate the

---

*Rambam* (Ramat Gan, 1983), pp. 154ff. See also Y. Ben-Sasson on R. Meir Simha of Dvinsk in *Sefer ha-Zikkaron le-Mordekhai Vizer* (Kevutzat Yavneh, 1981), pp. 346–66 (Heb.).

[28] See *Shiurim*, p. 130 and n. 14; this comment, incidentally, is of special relevance to our discussion.

normative calendar: "Now, *Knesset Israel* in its entirety sanctifies . . ., the holidays and New Moons by its ritual practice. . . . The entire people fixes the calendar through the calculations, and the celebration of the holidays and New Moons according to these calculations functions to set the calendar." And in a charming aside, the Rav explains the familiar phrase in the synagogal announcement of the New Moon, *haverim kol Yisrael* (in the comradeship of all Israel) as no rhetorical flourish, but rather as the liturgical statement of our doctrine.[29]

Halakhic theory, it thus seems, accommodates the changed reality of the Jewish people very well. Yet from another perspective, the theory spun out above reflects an ideal situation; or in terms more familiar from *Halakhic Man,* it expresses the *a priori.* For if this theory absorbs with little shock the reality of a destroyed Temple, and an abolished Sanhedrin, it is predicated on the assumption of an ideal people, a people that observes the Sabbaths and holy days of the year as of yore. But we all know—and so does R. Soloveitchik—that "the entire people" no longer celebrates the holidays. The theory, indeed, seems appropriate for a premodern age, for a people that exists as a memory. What now?

At this point, of course, we enter the realm of the speculative. A number of options ought to be raised, then. The Rav may think, for one thing, that even if the majority of the people no longer sanctifies the holidays in a halakhic mode, it does recognize them as its own. Don't most Jews continue to identify with Pesah, for example? A possible implication of this argument is that if even this bare identification were to be restricted to a minority, the people would no longer have a calendar, for which the legitimation of the entire *Knesset Israel* is necessary. This would be radical doctrine indeed, as the pious minority would then be unable to function, abandoned as it were by the mass of the Jewish people! The opposing alternative, of course, is to assume that the Rav recognizes the observant minority itself as *Knesset Israel,* the remnant that becomes the "entire people." Actually, none of these options seems terribly convincing. Rather we retreat to the admission that no "solution" exists, and we discuss matters on a different level.

---

[29] Ibid., pp. 130–31; see also p. 228.

Put plainly, we must admit that R. Soloveitchik here seems to be writing pure halakhic theory, as he explicates Talmud and Maimonides, which are read as ideal texts. And he rests his case on an ideal understanding of the Jewish people as a nation of purpose and destiny. Jewry as a nation of historical fate and nothing more simply does not enter the picture. *Hurban ha-bayit* has, in a sense, been absorbed into this theoretical model; *hurban ha-Am* has not. A terrible chasm does, in fact, exist between halakhic theory and modern reality: theory simply refuses to grasp reality. But something more ought to be added.

Halakhic theory, in this case at least, is perhaps more than analytic description. It is also a statement of faith. Here (and elsewhere), the Rav asserts that the Jewish people, which is incomprehensible to him outside its covenantal commitment, will return to its vocation of holiness. Messianic faith, he declares, is "faith in the Jewish people."[30] Thus, despite the two-tiered historical model of "Kol Dodi Dofek," no halakhic model exists for a bifurcated Jewish people. The Jewish people is ever Sinai, Torah. (Interestingly, the halakhic theory behind the workings of the calendar also led Maimonides to one of his more daring statements of faith when he asserted that the Lord would never allow the Land of Israel to be totally emptied of its Jews. That, he wrote, is a concomitant of God's commitment to the ongoing existence of His people.[31]) Ironically, it is precisely the description of the authority immanent in Jewish life that suggests how far contemporary Jewish life actually is from its sacred vocation, and the argument for the indispensability of this authority, which suggests how fragile the sacred existence of this people is today. The calendar—at least on the theory developed by the Rav—is living on borrowed time, and not the calendar alone.

## V

The very being of the Jewish people is inextricably tied up for the Rav with Torah. Usually the people is identified with Oral Law, rather than Written Law.

---

[30] *On Repentance*, pp. 132–37.

[31] *Sefer ha-Mitzvot, Aseh* 153.

In its power and authority to decide halakhic issues—an authority greater than that of the scholars, whose decisions are based on intellectual grounds alone—is expressed the mystic, holy, idea, that Torah and Israel are one.[32]

Israel is holy because it is identical with Torah, because Israel is itself Torah and Torah is itself Israel.[33]

The force of the identification with Oral Law specifically seems to be that Torah is then immanent within the people itself, rather than being an external standard alone, which is what the Written Law apparently symbolizes. The latter statement cited explains, in context, why the Jewish people, however sinful, remains eternal.[34] But rather than exploit this idea to the fullest degree, R. Soloveitchik continues to say that the Torah as Oral Law is always within the people because "the mind and memory, the very soul of the Jew, contains hidden myriads of letters and crowns of the tradition: bits of prayer, memories of a festival . . . echoes of a Torah-idea. . . . there always remains a divine spark which cannot be profaned." And while it is true that R. Soloveitchik speaks here of "authority to decide halakhic issues," the Rav is actually quite far from the modernist exploitation of this identity as a basis for innovation. Many modernists, of course, value the idea of the immanent authority of the community precisely as it counters and dislodges the normative tradition. This is simply not the drift of R. Soloveitchik's discussion. For the Israel of which he speaks is still the ideal people of purpose discovered in our discussion of the calendar, and the Torah of which he speaks was given at Sinai. The two basic foci of the identity of Israel and Torah, then, are that (1) Israel is a community whose positive historic continuity has been forged through the study and teaching of Torah, and (2) alongside

---

[32] Joseph B. Soloveitchik, *Yemei Zikkaron*, trans., Moshe Kroner (Jerusalem: World Zionist Organization, 1986), p. 59.

[33] Ibid., p. 249.

[34] As Rabbi Soloveitchik indicates (Ibid., p. 247), the terms of this distinction and its application to the Jewish people are found in *Beit ha-Levi* (Homily XVIII); interestingly the issue of the sinfulness of the people is not raised in that context.

the tradition of study there has always flowed the experience of the life
of Torah itself. Indeed, the Rav finds the tension and complementarity
of the intellectual and the experiential a fascinating and charged topic.
The sensitivity to this problematic does not grow from a sense of the
gap between theory and the demands of the real world. Rather it grows
from a sense of the richness and variety of the spiritual experience, and
of the frustration encountered within the intellectual act. The limitations
of the intellectual experience will be felt, obviously, only by one who is
so fundamentally committed to it. Be this as it may, the story of Jewish
history is not, for the Rav, a tale of dislocations, discontinuities, gaps.
Rather, it is a conversation across the ages by generations linked not only
in common purpose but in common understanding. The passage of time
does not produce distance or alienation; rather, it adds partners to the
ever-enriched conversation. It is not necessary to add that, even casting
metaphysical assumptions aside, the question of what is history—How
is it to be perceived, written? What is significant in the record of the
past?—can only be answered in the most subjective way.

R. Soloveitchik frequently returns to the imagery of the community of the *massorah* (tradition), the community whose continuity is
the essence of Oral Law. This continuity is represented, of course, in
the experience of "learning;" which is an intensely personal, indeed
emotional, experience:

> When I sit down to learn Torah, I find myself immediately in
> the company of the sages of the *massorah*. The relations be-
> tween us are personal. The Rambam is at my right, Rabbenu
> Tam at my left, Rashi sits up front and interprets, Rabbenu
> Tam disputes him; the Rambam issues a ruling, and the Rabad
> objects. They are all in my little room, sitting around my table
> . . . Torah study is not solely an educational activity. . . . It is
> a powerful experience of becoming friends with many genera-
> tions of Torah scholars, the joining of one spirit with another,
> the union of souls. Those who transmitted Torah and those
> who received it come together in one historical way-station. [35]

[35] *And From There You Shall Seek* (Jersey City, 2008), p. 145. See now Michael Oppenheim,
"Kierkegaard and Soloveitchik," *Judaism* 37, 1 (Winter, 1988), pp. 38–39, who points out

Or again:

> . . . the massorah society was founded by Moses at the dawn of
> our history and at the point of eschatological fulfillment of our
> history will be joined by the King Messiah.[36]

What characterizes that society? An unqualified dedication to
learning and teaching, its motto is teach and let yourself be taught.
It demands that every Jew be simultaneously teacher and pupil, that
every member of the society hold on with one hand to an old teacher
while the other hand rests upon the frail shoulders of a young pupil.
This society that represents the very essence of Judaism cuts across the
ages and millennia and holds the key to our miraculous survival.

On the long Sabbath afternoons in the summer, we preface the re-
cital of *Pirke Avot* with a declaration concerning our total involvement
in the *massorah* community: "Moses received the Torah from Sinai, and
handed it on to Joshua, and Joshua to the Elders, and the Elders to the
Prophets, and the Prophets handed it on to the men of the Great As-
sembly." In other words, Judaism expresses itself through the *shalshelot
ha-kabbalah,* the chain of tradition. Hands are linked; generations are
united. One society encompasses past, present, and future. As mentioned before, admission to that society is a difficult and complex affair.

Though open to all, and even demanding that all enter, this society
is admittedly elitist. At the same time, it is not peripheral to Jewish
peoplehood. Indeed, one senses that for R. Soloveitchik, this society is
the very essence of Jewish community; in it and through it does one
discover the meaning of Jewish commitment.

There is another aspect to the *massorah* community, and the Rav
is careful to insist on this second reality. It forms part of the community of the tradition but does not contribute to its intellectual
substance. Occasionally R. Soloveitchik will identify it again on a
personal level-with dominant maternal figures; on other occasions it

---

that participation in the chain of the *massorah* community is, for the Rav, an answer to the
ravages of time.

[36] "Tribute to the Rebbitzen of Talne," *Tradition* 17:2 (Spring, 1978), pp. 75–76. Available at
www.traditiononline.org.

is embodied in the people as a whole, which bears the responsibility for the concretization of Jewish commitment through history. There is, on the one hand, his description of his mother and of the *rebbitzen* of Talne:[37]

> People are mistaken in thinking that there is only one massorah and one massorah community; the community of the fathers. It is not true. We have two massorot, two traditions, two communities, two *shalshalot ha-kabbalah*—the massorah community of the fathers, and that of the mothers. "Thus shalt thou say to the house of Jacob (the women) and tell the children of Israel (the men)" (Exodus 19:3), "Hear my son the instruction of thy father (*mussar avikha*) and forsake not the teaching of thy mother (*torat imekha*)" (Proverbs 1:18), counseled the old king. . . .
>
> I admit that I am not able to define precisely the massoretic role of the Jewish mother. Only by circumscription I hope to be able to explain it. Permit me to draw upon my own experiences. I used to have long conversations with my mother. In fact, it was a monologue rather than a dialogue. She talked and I "happened" to overhear. What did she talk about? I must use an halakhic term in order to answer this question; she talked *me-inyana de-yoma.* I used to watch her arranging the house in honor of a holiday. I used to see her recite prayers; I used to watch her recite the sidra every Friday night and I still remember the nostalgic tune. I learned from her very much.
>
> Most of all, I learned that Judaism expresses itself not only in formal compliance with the law but also in a living experience. She taught me that there is a flavor, a scent and warmth to *mitzvot.* I learned from her the most important thing in life— to feel the presence of the Almighty and the gentle pressure of His hand resting on my frail shoulders. Without her teachings,

---

[37] Ibid.

which quite often were transmitted to me in silence, I would have grown up a soulless being, dry and insensitive.

The laws of Shabbat, for instance, were passed on to me by my father; they were part of *mussar avikha*. The Shabbat as a living entity, as a queen, was revealed to me by my mother; it is a part of *torat imekha*. The fathers *knew* much about the Shabbat; the mothers *lived* the Shabbat, experienced her presence and perceived her beauty and splendor.

The fathers taught generations how to observe the Shabbat; mothers taught generations how to feel the Shabbat and how to enjoy her twenty-four hour presence.

The Rebbitzen, as I mentioned before, was one of the few women to whom the maternal *massorah, torat imekha,* was entrusted. She represented the *massorah* community with great loyalty and dedication. She was a devoted, good keeper of the treasure that was put in escrow with her and she knew how to guard it and how to transmit it to another generation. She was an outstanding teacher.

Now, this description dovetails perfectly with the Rav's analysis of the two forms of traditional authority: that of scholarly analysis and decision, and that of life lived by the people itself. Needless to say, the midrash kabbalistic imagery of *Knesset Israel* should be recalled, as well.[38] And though the essay devoted to this idea is in fact titled "Two Forms of *Massorah*," there is, again, no indication that the authority immanent in Israel's experience is perceived as in conflict with its normative heritage; nor is there much interest in discussion of this problematic.[39] Though not identical, experience and norm flow in the same direction and supplement, rather than conflict with, each other. (Needless to say, any analysis of Rabbi Soloveitchik's halakhic posture will also have to take into account his responsiveness to modern reality—a phenomenon

[38] *Berakhot* 35b; *Pesahim* 50b; *Hullin* 93b.
[39] *Shiurim*, pp. 220–40.

that does not come to the fore in his published writings.) This, then, is the second component of community as Oral Law: the community whose very life is an ongoing embodiment of Torah.

It is through this massoretic community—in both its aspects—that the Jew finds God:

> The individual and the community must come together through an act of historical identification with the past and future, the fate and destiny, of the Jewish people. . . . Thus can the individual cleave completely and absolutely to God . . . [40]

Once again, the individual and his quest are the center of concern. And once again, the Jewish individual can attain his ultimate goal only with the community of Jews, past, present and future.

Interestingly, the Rav opens two avenues of *devekut* in *U-Vikkashtem mi-Sham,* an essay devoted largely to the possibility and modes of communion with God. There is *devekut* through the study of Torah in which, as Ravitzky has shown,[41] the Torah shared by man and God creates an epistemological basis for communion. But there is also *devekut* through ethical behavior within the community, though its theoretical basis is less developed and though this community, the Rav insists, is the committed covenantal community alone.[42]

In the passage cited above, which is virtually at the close of the essay, Rabbi Soloveitchik apparently collapses this distinction.[43]

---

[40] *And From There You Shall Seek*, pp. 147–48. One wonders whether the terms *goral* and *ye'ud* ("fate" and "destiny"), used here in a work roughly contemporary with *Halakhic Man*, have the same meaning as would be assigned them in "Kol Dodi Dofek." If so, we see the fusion of concern for the two communities. See also below at the conclusion of this essay.

[41] Aviezer Ravitzky. "Kinyan ha-Da'at be-Haguto," in *Sefer Yovel li-Khevod Morenu ha-Gaon Yosef Dov ha-Levi Soloveitchik*, pp. 138–40.

[42] *And From There You Shall Seek*, p. 89. Remarkably, the Rav's discussion takes as its point of departure the rabbinic dictum to "adhere to the sages"; Rabbi Soloveitchik chooses to take his saying as directing the Jew to his community, rather than to the masters of Torah. See also Ravitzky, pp. 146–51.

[43] Though our citation seemingly focuses on the community and its history alone, these sentences conclude a discussion of the role of prophets and sages.

# "Fate" and "Destiny"

In the previous chapter we dealt with the concepts of "covenant of fate" and "covenant of destiny" as providing a way of absorbing Jews who are not committed to the Sinaitic covenant in the Jewish community. We note that such integration is quite understandable from a halakhic perspective and that it also has roots in Aggadah. We also allude to more modern conceptual sources, especially to the *Bet ha-Levi's* sixteenth sermon that distinguishes between "God's children" and "God's people."

The categories chosen by the Rav also functioned in modern thought of his time and place.

In 1921, Martin Buber delivered his lecture "On Nationalism" at the World Zionist Congress which convened in Carlsbad.[1] Buber distinguishes there between "people" (*Volk*) and "nation":

> The concept "people" always implies unity of fate. It presupposes that . . . throngs of human beings were shaped into a new entity by a great molding fate they experienced in common. . . . The spiritual factor is an organic, potential, common memory which becomes actual in each successive generation as the pattern for experience, as language, and as a way of life. The people constitutes a particular sort of community . . .

> A people becomes a nation to the degree that it grows aware that its existence differs from that of other peoples . . . conscious

---

[1] This lecture was published in 1936 in his book, *Zion als Zeil und als Aufgabe*, pp. 78–87, and also appeared in 1948 in English in a collection of his essays: Martin Buber, *Israel and the World* (New York, 1948), pp. 214–28.

and active difference. Historically speaking, this consciousness is usually the result of some inner—social or political—transformation, through which the people comes to realize its own peculiar structure and actions, and sets them off from those of others. It is a decisive activity and suffering . . . which produces a *people*. A *nation* is produced when its acquired status undergoes a decisive inner change which is accepted as such in the people's self-consciousness.

Buber distinguishes here between two layers of national existence (in this he is at one with European nationalist thought in general, as was noted by Nathan Rotenstreich.[2] One layer is based on a shared "fate," that is, historical pressure, suffering, but also cultural activity and even innovation, such as language and way of life. The second layer, in contrast, is based on *internal consciousness*, and this is what establishes the "nation."

Buber illustrates these concepts in Jewish history:

A great event in their history molded the Jews into a people. It was when the Jewish tribes were freed from the bondage of Egypt. But it required a great inner transformation to make them into a nation. In the course of this inner change, the concept of the government of God took on a political form . . . the kingdom as the representative of God. . . .

"Fateful" reality is what fashioned the *people* of Israel, whereas an inner-spiritual experience is what created the *nation*. The exodus from Egypt and the Sinaitic covenant represent moments in the history of the people-nation.

There are striking differences between Buber's outlook and that of R. Soloveitchik, both conceptual and practical. According to Buber, the *people* fashioned by "fate" forms for itself a cultural mold and way of life; a *nation* reaches a level of consciousness, but not a qualitatively

---

[2] Nathan Rotenstreich, *HaMahashava HaYehudit BaʿEt HaHadasha*, 3rd printing, I (Tel Aviv, 1987), pp. 180, 265–70 (not found in English translation).

different creative level. This activity also exists for the Rav, with respect to the solidarity established among slaves and the like, but nevertheless the difference is clear. According to Buber, the struggle with fate is active, whereas according to R. Soloveitchik, the people formed by way of a covenant of fate is fundamentally passive. This broad distinction expresses itself in the fact that for Buber, the decisive fateful moment was the exodus from Egypt, whereas R. Soloveitchik focuses on the Egyptian bondage itself.

Regarding the last point, the Rav clearly draws here upon the trauma of the destruction of European Jewry, which once again proved that the fate of the people is realized in historical suffering, and not in dizzying liberation. The inner experience as well, as common as it may be to both Buber and R. Soloveitchik, is slightly different. Buber also alludes to the giving of the Torah at Sinai. But for him, this covenant is not halakhic in the sense that it is understood by the Rav, but rather ideological.

However, in order to fully understand Buber's position, one must go to the end of the lecture, where Buber continues:

Judaism is not merely being a nation. It is being a nation, but because of its own peculiar connection with the quality of being a community of faith, it is more than that. . . . In Judaism . . . membership in a community of faith. From the French Revolution on, this inner bond grew more and more insecure. Jewish religion was uprooted. . . . Over and over this nationalism lapses into trends toward "secularization" and thus mistakes its purpose. For Israel cannot be healed . . . by severing the concepts of people and community of faith. . . .

Here the question may arise as to what the idea of the election of Israel has to do with all this. This idea does not indicate a feeling of superiority, but a sense of destiny. It does not spring from a comparison with others, but from the concentrated devotion to a task, to the task which molded the people into a nation . . .

Here we already hear about "destiny," destiny that serves as the foundation for the transformation of the Jews from a *people* to a *nation*. (Buber continues with the argument that it is only clinging to destiny that will save Jewish nationalism from turning the people into the object of idol worship.) This destiny finds expression, of course, in the giving of the Torah.

It is difficult not to conclude that we are dealing with two conceptual worlds that closely converge upon each other, worlds that even find expression in similar terminology. But whereas Buber deals with the problem of pathological nationalism that overran Europe on the eve of the twentieth century, and which was also spreading, in his opinion, in the Jewish community, Rabbi Soloveitchik deals with a different problem: how to understand modern Jewish existence, how to find an authentic conceptual parallel to the complexity of historical reality, in the creation of the State of Israel and the secularization of considerable portions of the nation. Therefore, and also owing to the penetration of the consciousness of the Holocaust into the Rav's thought, "the covenant of fate" is defined for him in a most minimalist fashion from a moral perspective, almost like preserving the body until the soul is returned to it.

An examination of the writings of another German-Jewish thinker reveals the use of similar terms and a preoccupation with partially similar problems, the reference here being to Prof. Alexander Altmann. He and Rabbi Soloveitchik both studied at the University of Berlin in the late 1920s, attended many of the same philosophy courses for several years, met almost daily, and engaged in long conversations as they strolled in Berlin's Tiergarten.[3]

Altman borrows the concepts of "*Schicksal*" (fate) and "*Erbe*" (heritage) from Heidegger, but it seems that he uses them in a slightly different sense. In any case, he emphasizes the "external fate," that is, the historical fate of the people:

---

[3] This information is taken from Prof. Paul Mendes-Flohr's introduction to a volume of Altmann's essays, *The Meaning of Jewish Existence*, ed. Alfred L. Ivry (Brandeis University Press), p. xviii. We get the impression that Prof. Altmann himself was the source of this information. Note should, of course, be taken of their joint interest in the writings of Max Scheler. Altmann wrote the essay, "*Was ist Judische Theologie?*" in 1933, and it appeared in English translation in the aforementioned volume, pp. 40–57.

It is the function of Jewish destiny in its tragic singularity to see to it that this claim of actuality be heard. The path leads from Jewish destiny to heeding ever anew what has been revealed. For this destiny . . . is itself revealed, and possesses a theological quality. Thus, there is revealed to the Jewish individual, the bearer of Jewish destiny, the always new call of God. . . . From this destiny there is only an either/or: The way into the darkness of impotent despair, i.e., retreat into immanence; or the way into the light, the thrust into the Jewishly experienced theological sphere. However, this way does not proceed from the individual; it proceeds only from the discovery of his peoplehood. . . .

These words were written after Hitler's rise to power, and as Mendes-Flohr notes there, this fact is engraved on almost every page. We are dealing with a "covenant of fate," not as it reflected itself after the Holocaust, but before it. Accordingly, Altmann can characterize Jewish fate as "tragic and joyful," as leading to "invigorating meaning that bestows revelation."

There are, of course, clear differences between Altmann and Rabbi Soloveitchik: Altmann does not interpret "fate" internally, as a bestowal of legitimacy upon the Jew who has not yet reached Sinai, but rather outwards—against the Church and a theological interpretation that does not deal with the historical-national element of Jewish existence. Altmann also narrows the gap between the historical moment and the moral one, as the one "leads" to the other, and revelation already lies concealed in historical fate. Rabbi Soloveitchik, on the other hand, emphasizes the breadth and depth of the gap, though he too is convinced about the uniqueness of Jewish historical fate.

However, despite these distinctions, we are dealing with similar national existential tension. The concepts were in the air, as the words of both Buber and Altmann testify. After the Holocaust, and in light of the national-religious problem with which the Rav struggled—the secularization and the sharing on the part of all branches of the nation in the tragic fate of modern Jewish history, on the one hand, and the dominant role played by the secular sector in the establishment of the

State of Israel, on the other. These concepts were renewed and developed, loaded with weighty and significant ideological meaning, and placed in the Jewish public domain by Rabbi Soloveitchik.[4]

---

[4] The attentive reader has no doubt noted that "*schiksal*" has been rendered as both "fate" and "destiny" in some of these materials. This reflects, I believe, the varied meanings attached to this term. At times, it has denoted a situation in which the people play a passive role; in other instances it signifies an invitation to active intervention. Here is how Martina Urban describes the situation: "The term *schiksal*, destiny, had been in vogue since the eve of World War I. . . . *Schiksal*, understood as fate, had come to portend a tragic vision of history. But with Heidegger, the *schiksalsbegriff*, or concept of destiny, possessed a positive, existential inflection. . . . Heidegger identified the "existential problem of historicity and . . . refashioned the concept of "destiny." . . . For Heidegger, destiny (*schicksal*) . . . emerges from one's historicity and takes the form of a resolute choice.. . . Destiny is thus not imposed by history; it is an existential moment in which a people affirms one of the possibilities of its historicity" (Matina Urban, "Persecution and the Art of Representation", in Idit Dobbs-Weinstein, Lenn E. Goodman and James A. Grady, eds., *Maimonides and His Heritage* [SUNY, 2009], pp. 157–58). R. Soloveitchik is closer to the pre-Heideggerian usage. It should also be noted that for a religious thinker (such as the Rav), "fate" too (and even more so, *goral*) is an expression of the divine will and not simply the moral equivalent of a coincidence or an arbitrary event. This last point is amply explicated by Rabbi Soloveitchik in his *Days of Deliverance*, eds. Eli D. Clark, Joel B. Wolowelsky and Reuven Ziegler, (KTAV, 2007), pp. 12–15.

# The Covenant of Marriage

The soul is overcome and shattered by fierce longing. Just before Rosh Hashanah, I imagined that my father, of blessed memory, was standing beside me. He was the one and only rebbi, master and teacher, that I ever had. I put down my life before him and said . . . But I knew that my beloved father, who had once been so close to me, was now far away, and my heart burst with the desire to talk to him for even five minutes . . . The same is true regarding my mother and my wife. . . . I asked, but I heard no reply.[1]

These remarks reflect the yearnings and feelings of guilt and loss that visit a person when God removes Himself from his life. But it is impossible to ignore the tempestuous personal emotions that burst out from these words. During the week that the Rav was sitting shiva for his wife, he wondered how halakhah could have limited the mourning rites observed for a spouse to thirty days (as opposed to twelve months for a parent). He introduced his monumental essay, *The Lonely Man of Faith,* with a detailed dedication to his wife, a dedication that was omitted from the Hebrew translation published in Israel in an act of literary vandalism, apparently as a gesture of political-religious correctness. He dedicated his major halakhic works that were published during his lifetime to his father: *Shiurim le-Zekher Abba Mari, z"l.*

The volume *Family Redeemed: Essays on Family Relationships*[2] is the intellectual correlative to this world of feelings. The six essays in this

---

[1] *On Repentance*, p. 280.

[2] Joseph B. Soloveitchik, *Family Redeemed: Essays on Family Relationships*, eds. David Shatz and Joel B. Wolowelsky (Toras HoRav Foundation, 2000). Page references in parentheses in this chapter are to that volume.

work are dedicated to marital and parental relationships as a Jewish and human phenomenon. It seems to me that the very writing of these essays during the late 1950s, the surprising decision to devote so much attention to the problems and challenges of marriage and family life, is in itself of great significance for understanding the Rav's world and personality. There is even a certain daring to this choice, as the Rav does not refrain from relating to the erotic component of the marital union. I am not familiar with another Jewish treatment of the issue similar to the one found in this book; a gaping divide stands between it and contemporary religious writing dealing with marriage. The raw materials of the discussion are taken from the world of Jewish tradition and experience, but it is meant to shed light upon the situation of every person. This illumination is based upon existential, psychological, and moral values, that is, universal values, and not on the unique "sanctity of Israel," which constitutes a central value in contemporary religious discourse in Israel.

According to R. Soloveitchik, marital union stands at the heart of the stories of the creation of man in the book of Genesis. Though in the first account of man's creation, the sexual union of the characters, referred to here as male and female, serves the biological/social objective of procreation ("be fruitful and multiply"), the second account focuses on the dependency relationships between the characters, who are now designated man and woman. This story points to the ontological loneliness of the person, the existential state that characterizes both man and woman: "It is not good that the man be alone" applies to all human beings. Marriage is the redeeming answer to this ontological loneliness, loneliness stemming both from man's alienation from the world of nature that surrounds him and from the need to find a spouse with whom he/she can develop a deep attachment.

The Rav argues that marriage, and no other interpersonal relationship, provides the solution, because it is founded on a covenant. This covenant, like the covenant between the people and God, implies total commitment and constancy, and not just contractual partnership. The vitality of a relationship anchored in a covenant does not stem from the fact that it implements a Divine command, but rather from the fact that it "creates a personal experience that enriches and enhances the lives of two individuals" (32). R. Soloveitchik was, as we know, one of the most prominent Jewish thinkers illuminating the concept of the covenant and its significance, though he usually dealt with the covenant as a theological concept. Here the Rav presents the anthropological content of the concept, while explaining the subjective meaning of this objective, halakhic norm. An echo of Buber enters in this discussion, but unlike Buber, the Rav is adamant in his belief that these precious interpersonal values are created and maintained precisely in a normative framework. (In addition to the similarity to the writings of Buber, the literary atmosphere and the nature of the connection to the book of Genesis bring to mind the second volume of Karl Barth's *Church Dogmatics*).

This covenantal relationship is founded on love, by means of which man is redeemed from "the distressing feeling of an incomplete lonely existence" (41). These feelings of love are nurtured by sexual activity, which leads to "making two free individuals depend upon and help each other" (51). For this reason, by the way, Judaism rejects, according to the Rav, the sacramental model of marriage: marriage does not need supernatural or sacerdotal approval of its legitimacy. Though he does not say this, the absence of sacrament is what makes divorce possible, a problem with which the book tries to contend. One should not expect, however, that love alone, and all the more so sexual activity by itself, will provide real meaning to the marital union. First of all, sexual activity by itself risks the guilt of depersonalization. And second, love is not necessarily identical with the commitment of monogamous marriage; it is possible to love more than one person. However, the moment that marriage as an objective norm takes its rightful place, the Rav can speak of a couple's love as "contact with the thou [that] bolsters [one's] own ego" (55).

Marriage, which sets an ethical norm, is the institution most appropriate to heal—in part—the existential human wound. Marriage is first and foremost a covenant, and as such it has the intensity, the depth, and the constancy that characterize the covenant between God and the people of Israel. The Rav adopts this model from the words of Malachi, who referred to a man's wife as "your companion, your covenanted wife" (Malachi 2:14), a metaphor in which one can find an echo of motifs from Genesis. A covenantal partnership is so obligating

in the Rav's eyes that he devotes several pages to justifying the institution of divorce, an issue with which Jewish thought usually has no
problem. (Without a doubt, the Rav is aware here, and also in other
places of the book, of the competing Christian model, and he wish-
es to set out the opposing Jewish model.) It should be remembered,
however, that the prophet defends "the wife of your covenant" precisely in the context of the divorce of "the wife of your youth, against
whom you have dealt treacherously" (ibid.). Both in ancient times and
in the medieval period the freedom to grant a divorce was not always
self-evident, whether for reasons of principle or circumstance. In any
event, the issue does not preoccupy contemporary Jewish thought, for
understandable reasons.

Marriage requires, first and foremost, mutual sacrifice. The reference, of course, is to the creation of an existential space in which the
couple can live both together and as separate individuals. But marriage involves sacrifice in another sense as well. The two parties must
sacrifice sexual freedom: first, with a decision in favor of monogamy
and fidelity, and second, in marital life itself, where total abstinence is
demanded at the time of the woman's monthly period. Here Judaism
formulates "strict laws . . . which drastically reduce the sexual activity
of the couple" (50). I do not find that the Rav adopted the approach
favored by contemporary religionists (which has a Talmudic foundation), who argue that sexual abstinence comes to renew erotic love. According to the Rav at issue is simple and painful abstinence that leads
to catharsis. Such an approach appears frequently in his writings.

However, despite this sexual sacrifice, covenantal marriage is "plea-
sure-oriented," and it is supposed to be that way. Marriage that does
not provide "carnal enjoyment and erotic love" (50) is to be dissolved.
We are dealing here not only with a normative contractual commitment—though the Rav elaborates on the halakhah regarding the mutual rights and obligations of physical gratification—but also with a
fundamental component of human marriage.

The Rav's preoccupation with the erotic component of the marital relationship certainly deviates from the norm of religious writing.
A long essay in this collection, "The Redemption of Sexual Life," is
entirely dedicated to the issue of sexuality, in addition to its treatment

in the essays on Adam and Eve and on marriage. The Rav deals in detail with a path that leads from vulgar and perverse sexuality, through readiness for withdrawal and self-restraint, to eroticism that serves as a foundation for the perfection of man. It is important to note that the Rav's negative attitude toward the sexual act as such does not stem, for the most part, from an ascetic or Augustinian inclination, but primarily from the inferior moral standing of the act, the aggression and depersonalization with which it is often accompanied. Accordingly, the Rav argues that Judaism is not ambivalent about sexuality; it just evaluates its objectives meticulously and selectively. The picture, in any case, is complex and multinuanced.

Despite the importance that the Rav assigns to a couple's love, romantic love included ("Love is an enriching, meaning-giving, and uplifting experience . . . The lack of it might shatter a life" [55]), the value of the covenant of marriage does not express itself only in the sexual relationship. "Covenantal marriage is a natural procreative community" (52). The normative command, "Be fruitful and multiply," returns in the form of "and they become one flesh" in the second story of creation, an expression that means, according to one understanding, that the two parties bring a third person into the world. We are not dealing with a biological or social function, but with the breach of the couple's egocentrism and subjectivism in order to bestow existence and love upon a third party that does not yet exist.

The Rav repeatedly emphasizes that it is only this readiness—which is sometimes described in nonbiological terms—that redeems the marital relationship and even sexuality. Through giving, love, and responsibility, man imitates his Creator. All this despite the fact that this third party will one day leave the nest and destroy the original triad: "That is why a man leaves his father and his mother, and cleaves to his wife." The Rav has few illusions about a relationship stemming exclusively from biology, void of moral foundations. In this, I heard him say, lies the educational importance of the Torah's legislation concerning a rebellious son, "*ben sorer*." Biological fatherhood "is doomed to failure, because [the father] never develops the proper relationship with his offspring" (122). A certain tension between the various essays can, however, be felt regarding this point: in some places, the marital union itself redeems, while in others, a third party is necessary.

* * *

Is Judaism reflected in these accounts? From where were the building-stones taken upon which the Rav bases his discussion? We shall not trace here the non-Jewish sources that were important to the Rav. Some are explicitly identified, others are hinted at, and still others lie deep within the structure. The essays are spiced with medieval Latin ecclesiastical terms, this wording omitted from the Hebrew translation (apparently to make the material more accessible to the reader, and perhaps also as a gesture to the religious community that is not comfortable in that cultural milieu), but we are talking about essential categories of thought. My question, in any event, is directed at the Jewish component of this unconventional book: Upon what is it based?

As one might expect from the author of *Halakhic Man,* halakhic sources are not lacking in this book. We have seen how the Rav refers to the laws of abstention and the duty to procreate—clear halakhic norms. The concept of a covenant in its broadest sense is also present in ancient as well as modern Jewish thought. The Rav expands upon the filial obligation to honor and fear one's parents, an issue that draws on halakhic sources. These are only a few examples. There is, however, a certain problem with the link to halakhic tradition as it is found in this collection of essays.

Covenantal marriage, as the Rav describes it, is based on mutuality—the mutual need for a spouse, the mutual search for a partner, and the mutuality of living together. At day's end, the description is one of love that accords with the romantic model, and goes beyond it. This marriage is monogamous in the deepest sense. It obligates the two sides/partners in equal measure, with all the ramifications and consequences of such a situation. This reality is essential for the moral-existential account given by the Rav. But can it be said that fundamental halakhah always maintained these demands?

The Rav seems to focus on two points. His first focus is the reality of the period within which he functions and towards which his words are directed. He speaks to a community located in a particular time and place, to the Jewish world, and perhaps to the world of the twentieth century in general. In this world, the woman suffers injury when a marriage dissolves or in the case of infidelity, but not in the course of a happy marriage. Second, he focuses on the stories of the Bible, and indeed, the Rav declares at the beginning of the book that Scripture is his source of guidance. The reference is primarily to the creation of Adam and Eve in the book of Genesis, which for him is a formative narrative.

For the Rav, the Genesis account dealing with primal man defines ideal human reality, a fairly commonplace idea in the history of the reading of that book (see the Midrash, the writings of Philo, and the Dead Sea scrolls). The stories of the patriarchs also strive towards that primal reality (that is, life with a single mate, though the patriarchs, apart from Isaac, do not succeed). The Rav's sociological-normative world is constructed in accordance with this model. Is it merely by coincidence that Judaism and human civilization in general have reached these norms, a reality that also allows for the moral-existential insight that may be inferred from it? Or are we dealing perhaps with the trajectory upon which human civilization moves, the trajectory that lies at the spiritual-existential foundations of humanity as they were set from the beginning? It seems that Rabbi Soloveitchik would have chosen the second alternative or something similar to it. Without a doubt, he would have seen halakhah, for the purpose of this discussion, as a historical compromise opposed to the ideal, as a floor rather than a ceiling. Indeed, the perception of halakhah as compromise was not alien to him.

*  *  *

The question of gender arises in the book in several contexts, both regarding marriage and regarding parenthood. We have already seen that, according to the Rav, the verse that defines man's existential dilemma, "It is not good that the man be alone," accords with the situation of every human being, man and woman alike. "There is no doubt that in the eyes of the halakhah man and woman enjoy an equal status and have the same worth as far as their *humanitas* is concerned" (71). And the Rav explains: both were created in God's image, both joined the covenantal community at Sinai, both are obligated to our historical destiny, and the like. According to him, misogyny, as is found in Hellenistic thought or as it appears in the writings of Schopenhauer, Weininger, Strindberg, and others has no place in Jewish tradition.

However, "the halakhah has discriminated between axiological equality . . . and metaphysical uniformity at the level of existential personal experience" (72). Each gender is "endowed with singular qualities and assigned distinct missions in life" (ibid.). The Rav even argues that the attraction of a member of one sex to a member of the other sex—a phenomenon that exists even among people who have already passed the age of full sexual activity—is based on the differences between them, on the lack of identity. Equality in qualities and missions, according to the Rav, harms romance. In other works, the Rav claims that even a woman's connection to Jewish tradition is different than that of a man: the *essence* of Shabbat, he remembers, he learned from his mother, whereas the *laws* of Shabbat he learned from his father.

The book includes descriptions based on the different inclinations of men and women, whether in relation to life in general, or in relation to their roles as parents. Even the formative account of Adam and Eve reveals, according to the Rav, different modes of action on the part of the two, differences that the Rav attributes to their difference in gender. The Rav also argues that the distinctions are typological, and that a biological male can embody the female type (he alludes that this is partly true of himself). But his descriptions are often rooted in biological reality (the effect of pregnancy on a woman's attitude toward her children), and all that we can say is that personality and biology are intertwined.

In light of this traditional attitude toward gender, I found great interest in the section that the volume's editors named: "The Tragedy in Motherhood." Indeed, the Rav himself uses the term "tragedy" in this context. In short, this assessment is based on the fact that Abraham (who sits "in front of the tent") responds to the angels' question, "Where is Sarah, your wife," with the answer, "Behold, in the tent," inside, concealed, without a public face, despite the importance of her work. The woman is found deep inside the tent, hidden, and her presence is passed on through her husband. Sarah's concealment—and that of all women—is not interpreted here in a favorable light. According to the Rav's homiletical reading of the passage, the dialogue between Abraham and the angels embodies the price that a woman must pay. The Rav reminds us that Abraham's historical role came to an end with Sarah's death, and that essentially each of the patriarchs left the stage with his wife's passing. The message is clear. "Why do not people know the truth" that Abraham's work was in large measure the work of Sarah? And yet, we say in our prayer, "God of Abraham," and not "God of Sarah," despite the fact that "they had an equal share in the Creator of the World." According to the Rav, it is here that "the tragedy manifests itself with all its impact." (120). The term "tragedy" is significant. The tragic is inherent, almost unpreventable, in reality—the human-social reality, or the religious-halakhic reality, as in our case. In any event, it is interesting to see how the Rav leads the homily to the halakhic realm, and in this realm—to prayer and its formulations, issues that were so close to his heart.

"Behind every successful man, there is a woman"—this saying notes both the critical importance of a woman and her concealment, and it is quite hackneyed. There is nothing special about its being adopted by the Rav, but his homiletics are quite interesting. Note should be taken of the critical tone that this recognition of women's fate raises against normative prayer, the readiness to consider and to justify—if only as a theoretical and emotional possibility—an alternative.

Honesty demands that we not translate these words—replete with personal elements—into a plan of action and an item on the religious community's agenda. The Rav also did not go further, in this unique passage, than to relate to the wording of the prayer. Is there any practical lesson to the declaration that a woman's life is tragic? In any event the Rav believes that life is filled with tragedy and suffering (which sometimes provides it with depth), and not infrequently it is impossible to frontally assault this essential misfortune. Accordingly, his declaration that a woman's life is partly tragic is not necessarily identical with a demand for halakhic reform. But even if the Rav does not give voice to a call for change, he does add here a different and surprising note to the traditional discussion. This note fits in well with the picture of the covenant of marriage portrayed throughout the book.

\* \* \*

Over the ten years that have passed since R. Soloveitchik's death, several collections of essays and homilies have been published based on notes and tapes of his lectures. At the same time, several volumes of halakhic studies were published: *Harerei Kedem,* on the festivals of Israel; *Reshimot Shiurim, Iggerot ha-Grid,* the extensive halakhic correspondence between the Rav and his father, Rabbi Moshe Soloveitchik; the *Sheurei HaRav* series published by the Orthodox Union; and various notebooks of *shi'urim.* These books contributed to the strengthening of the Rav's reputation as a profound and creative halakhic scholar—some even say the most profound halakhic scholar of the second half of the twentieth century. *Family Redeemed: Essays on Family Relationships* adds—for the first time in the last decade—an important dimension to the Rav as a thinker.

By placing this volume alongside the Rav's halakhic works, we are reminded once again of his uniqueness. Despite the recent attempts to blur and even sully this singularity, the written words speak for themselves.

# The Norms and Nature of Mourning

A not insignificant body of analysis, interpretation, and commentary has already been devoted to the Rav's writing and thought. Attention has been directed to the Rav's homiletic work as well as his topical writings, to be sure; much has been written about the Rav's view of man and of the people Israel. Nor have his discussions of the nature and ends of halakhah, his descriptions of the halakhic process and of how one "does" halakhah, been ignored either. We now have the beginnings of a serious discussion of the Rav's halakhic ideology, his conception of the relationship of halakhic thought to the world of physical and social phenomena, and of the relationship of halakhic conceptualization to the raw halakhic information available to the thinker.[1] Moreover, it is R. Soloveitchik's description of the halakhic process, his ideology of halakhah, if you will, that has stimulated the most trenchant criticism of his work, particularly as regards his denial of the historic character of the halakhic process and his pursuit of analogies drawn from the abstract world of mathematics—rather than from the human sciences—to describe the nature and goals of halakhah. This, of course, is how it should be, for halakhah was at the very center of the Rav's life and work.

Nonetheless, little has been done, I believe, in actual treatment of the Rav's specific halakhic studies. These, ostensibly, ought to be the best exemplars of the claims made in more general terms in the programmatic essays, in terms of both content and method. My rather modest intention, then, is to present Rabbi Soloveitchik's thinking on

---

[1] Lawrence Kaplan, "Rabbi Joseph B. Soloveitchik's Philosophy of Halakhah," *Jewish Law Annual* 7 (1988), pp. 139–98.

a specific topic, indeed to do not much more than provide a summary of his analysis and conclusions. Naturally, I will also say something about the methodological structure of the enterprise; and I will also try to provide some interpretation of the discussion, to make connections and to render the implicit, explicit. But I will hardly attempt to generalize about the Rav's halakhic method from the case at hand, except insofar as he himself does so. Nor will I attempt to suggest if and how this method departs from—or simply adopts—the method of other halakhists, or to comment on the relationship of the Rav's substantive conclusions with those of others.

The *shiurim* I shall discuss proceed in the traditional mode.[2] The Rav first assembles a list of textual anomalies and contradictions and then proceeds to solve the series of problems by presenting an overall thesis—analytical, of course, rather than textual or historical—which accounts for the earlier, puzzling phenomena. But if the structure is traditional, the exposition is not: the *shiurim* are expansive, not terse, in the classic style of halakhic writings. Nor is the reader left to form his own judgments; various rhetorical devices are used, points are elaborated, and one senses an attempt to convince. Perhaps the *shiurim* retain some characteristics of oral presentations, though they are also worked literary artifices.

Be this as it may, the literary structure of these essays is traditional. R. Soloveitchik begins with the problematic texts and then moves to the resolution and synthesis. This strategy indicates, at a most basic level,

---

[2] I would no longer characterize the Rav's *shiurim* given in memory of his father and subsequently published, as being in the traditional mode, or as traditional in structure. Most traditional work is anchored in a specific text, broadening out to other texts only as ramifications (or contradictions) of the initial source. Thus, it is hardly true (as I suggest below) that the traditional halakhic study assembles a list of anomalies and then proceeds to solve the problems by presenting an overall thesis. Traditional halakhic commentary, rather, tends to focus on single sources, interpreted through an initial, hypothetical thesis, which is then refined by the dialectical interpolation of more and more sources; this certainly characterizes the responsa literature as well. In these *shiurim* the rav, on the contrary, makes an initial presentation of numerous sources that require resolution in the guise of an overall thesis.

So we should speak of the Rav as author of path-breaking halakhic essays, in form no less than in content. As I shall point out shortly, both form and content (and their interrelationship) derive from the seriousness with which R. Soloveitchik approached his task as educator and conceptualizer of halakhic materials.

that the text or behavioral norm is primary—it is the given ground of all theory and discussion. Beginning with the problems is also fair to the listener, who can challenge any solution along the way or provide his own alternatives: he can be an active partner, not only a passive audience. My presentation of the Rav's work, however, will lean towards the more common style of academic work, as I shall focus quite quickly on the broad theses, though some of the textual material will be provided as well—as proof, if not as matrix. Why? In part, because I wish to make these materials accessible to those unaccustomed to the traditional style. But more broadly, because I wish to present the Rav's halakhic thought as a substantive, coherent statement about significant topics—not merely a series of glittering solutions to halakhic puzzles. So it is important to note that R. Soloveitchik himself reworks the conclusions of the Talmudic *shiurim* here considered into statements of halakhic phenomenology that are relatively detached from textual issues.[3]

I shall deal with R. Soloveitchik's discussion of mourning. This is a topic to which he returns on a number of occasions, but I shall focus on the two major essays found in *Shiurim le-Zekher Abba Mari*.[4]

## II

The first of our two essays deals with the obligation that priests render themselves impure on the death of any of the seven closest relatives, despite the general ban on priestly impurity. This imperative, R. Soloveitchik argues, is critically different from the apparently similar requirement that both priest and Nazirite—who is also required to avoid impurity—render themselves impure when they encounter an abandoned corpse *(met mitsvah)*. This impurity for the *met mitsvah* is functional; that is, it is a function of the obligation to bury this corpse, an act that entails contact and hence impurity. The impurity commanded

---

[3] Thus, compare the problem-oriented discussion in section 3, *infra*, with the synthetic discussion in *And From There You Shall Seek*, pp. 193–98, n. 19.

[4] *Shiurim le-Zekher Abba Mari*, *z"l*, I (Jerusalem, 1983), pp. 40–49; II, (Jerusalem, 1985), pp. 182–96. Avinoam Rosenack's interesting discussion of *aveilut* in the work of the Rav came to my attention after this essay had been prepared; see his *Hashpa'ot shel Modellim Filosofiyyim al haHashiva haTalmudit shel haRav . . . Soloveitchik* (Hebrew U., M. A. Thesis, 1994), pp. 104–16.

the priest for his relative, on the other hand, is substantive. In rendering himself impure for his closest relatives, the priest performs an act of ritual mourning. It is not, contrary to what one might assume, a function of the obligation to bury these relatives.[5]

This incisive distinction derives, first, from a close reading of the relevant texts. R. Soloveitchik notes that Maimonides, when describing the impurity commanded the priest/Nazirite for the abandoned corpse, always explicitly mentions its functional quality, saying that the priest/ Nazirite become impure so as to bury the corpse. This proviso is missing in descriptions of priestly impurity for relatives, and the Rav argues that this omission is pointed and deliberate. This distinction also serves to explain a number of halakhic anomalies.

First: one is required to bury even the heretic. But the priestly relative must not incur impurity on his death. All this dovetails with a third halakhic phenomenon, namely, that the death of the heretic does not entail mourning by his relatives. Thus, we see that impurity is a correlate of mourning, not burial. It is substantive rather than functional. My second example is more rewarding. The female priest is not required to render herself impure even though she is required to mourn. This is decidedly awkward for the Rav's thesis, as impurity now does not seem to be an aspect of mourning at all. R. Soloveitchik proceeds, however, to utilize just this situation to confirm and indeed deepen his thesis. For Maimonides himself explains that the female priest's exemption from the obligation of impurity is entailed by the fact that she—as distinct from the male priest—is generally not commanded to remain pure. R. Soloveitchik infers from this

---

[5] See R. Meir Simha of Dvinsk, *Or Same'ah* to *H. Avel* 3, 8. This understanding of mandated priestly impurity is extremely explicit in *Sefer ha-Mitsvot, Ase* 37 (which, surprisingly, the Rav does not cite), where such impurity is simply identified with the imperative of mourning and serves as its Scriptural base. In *H. Avel*, on the other hand, this nexus is somewhat weakened: the Scriptural status of the imperative of mourning is demonstrated through *Leviticus* 10:20 (see on), while priestly impurity serves more as argumentation (*H. Avel* 2, 6); this impurity, moreover, serves to underscore the importance that one "occupy oneself with (*she-yitasek*), and mourn for" the deceased, seemingly blurring the clear distinction between responsibility for burial and mourning. This blurring is even more accentuated in *H. Avel* 2, 7, where mandated impurity for a wife follows seamlessly after the impurity for other relatives, though she is explicitly described as *met mitsvah*—which implies that the impurity is functional, as we have seen—and the identical *la* (see n. 6) is used for her case as for the latter.

that impurity is an aspect of mourning only when it violates the priestly status; otherwise, as in the case of the female priest, it is not an act of mourning and is not required. So it is not impurity per se which is desired or which constitutes mourning, but rather the violation of priestly status that impurity accomplishes: this violation is the act of mourning.

Our distinction between the two imperatives of impurity leads to one final, most generative conclusion. R. Soloveitchik claims that since the impurity of the Nazirite is functional and goal oriented, it is mandated whenever it is necessary for the burial of the abandoned corpse; the Nazirite is expected to incur impurity through contact with sources of impurity other than the corpse itself if these must be moved, say, so as to bury the *met mitsvah*. For the priest, on the other hand, the mandated impurity is not functional at all, but substantive; it is an act of mourning to be performed only in connection with the body of his deceased relative.[6] This conclusion leads to the solution of problems that R. Soloveitchik placed at the very head of his essay, but I shall not pursue this intricate discussion here.

A major substantive implication of the Rav's discussion, one to which he is committed as part of his overall construction of mourning, is that contrary to the usual claim, mourning begins at the moment of death itself, not with the burial. It is only by assuming that mourning begins with death that the Rav can interpret priestly impurity as an aspect of mourning, for it is contracted before burial. Or, put differently: the successful analysis of priestly impurity as an act of mourning demonstrates that mourning begins before burial. Now, we shall return to a fuller discussion of this perspective, but

---

[6] I have not found an explicit Talmudic or Maimonidean statement to the effect that the impurity of the priest for his relative must be occasioned through contact with the body of the deceased relative itself (and given Rabbi Soloveitchik's understanding of the meaning of this commanded impurity, the point could be moot), but the Talmudic anecdotes on this topic all concern impurity generated in that way. Apparently the terms *lo* and *la* in the second chapter of *Hilkhot Avel* are to be taken as signifying "through him (or her)," not "for him (or her)." The discussion in *Semakhot* 3, 7, ed. Michael Higger, p. 118 (codified in *Hilkhot Avel* 2, 8), as to whether this impurity must be contracted before burial or even afterwards (a most interesting debate in its own terms) must then be understood as implying the option that the burial-cavern would be reopened so as to allow the priest to be contaminated, much as in the explicit anecdote following, where it is opened so that he may look at the deceased.

suffice it to say that it promises to illumine, both phenomenologically and psychologically, the normative experience of mourning.

What we have seen up to this point also enables us—indeed, it requires us—to probe the Rav's discussion from a methodological point of view. It should be apparent that the Rav has done more than distinguish between texts or practices only so as to iron out the apparent contradictions and anomalies they present. Rather, he has provided a distinction that attempts something much deeper. In essence, he has posed the question of the basic meaning and purpose of the halakhic norms at issue. The heart of R. Soloveitchik's distinction between the impurity commanded the priest/Nazirite and the priestly relative does not lie in the description of how each behaves but rather in the exploration of why each behaves as he does or the meaning of this behavior within the normative structure—for it is this meaning that controls and determines the behavior itself, though the details of the how support and express the grand theory of the why. In one case, as we have seen, we are dealing with a functional norm that serves to expedite burial; in the other, we are dealing with a performative aspect of mourning itself.

Now, this normative discourse is also very suggestive as a mode of both structuring and understanding human experience as it confronts death. It might imply, for example, that mourning requires loss of status as well as desanctification. Loss of status, in turn, might express self-abnegation in recognition of human impotence and mortality; desanctification, by preventing the priest's presence in the Temple, might express the mourner's removal from the presence of God, with all that that implies in turn. It should be clear that R. Soloveitchik does not himself make these interpretative suggestions in our essay (though he does elsewhere explore the halakhic aspects of the parallel notions that joy is a correlate of the presence of God just as grief is a correlate of His absence). His explicit topic here is the nature of priestly impurity. This is explored in terms of the halakhic rubric of mourning in a discussion that resolves numerous anomalies, thus transforming them into proofs of the thesis itself.

# III

The essay published in the second volume of *Shiurim le-Zekher Abba Mari,* directly confronts the performative norms of mourning as well as its essential internal correlates and manifestations, and represents the Rav's fullest discussion of *aveilut.* This discussion confronts a number of issues, including the obligation (or ban) of mourning on Sabbath and Festivals; the similarity and dissimilarity of mourning for the dead and the mourning-ritual adopted by the leper; the mourning-ritual of priests; and the differentiation of mourning behavior along its chronological axis. Now, in order to produce a coherent and coordinated understanding of these aspects of the mourning-performance, the Rav finds it necessary to present an analysis of mourning itself. Indeed, this very distinction between mourning-behavior and its grounding, and the concomitant demonstration that both behavior and internalization function normatively, would seem to be the matrix from which the rest of the analysis flows. These essays indicate that both performance and internalization are halakhic components of mourning. To be more specific: mourning requires both patterned ritual activity and individualized emotional activity, that is to say, grief. Though one may be expressive of the other, both are equally halakhic. The internalized activity, in other words, is not the "aggadic" correlate of the performed ritual. Rather, ritual and emotion are both normative; indeed, the interplay of the two is a basic given of halakhic discussion and dynamic. This, of course, is a claim that the Rav makes frequently.[7]

The normative interplay of behavior and internalization, ritual-mourning and grief, is most clearly apparent in the question of mourning ritual on Sabbath and Holidays. The halakhic situation posited here is that mourning is not practiced on Holidays, for the Talmud says, "The communal command to rejoice [or: The command to rejoice communally] overrules the individual's command to mourn [or: the command to mourn as an individual]." Now, mourning and holiday-ritual do not rule each other out as behavioral norms; it is possible

---

[7] See, e.g., *Al haTeshuva,* pp. 40–45, and elsewhere. Yizhak Gottlieb's useful paper, "*Al Gishato haHilkhatit shel haRav Y. D. Soloveitchik,*" *Shana beShana* 5754, pp. 186–97, came to my attention after the original article from which this chapter was taken was prepared.

to eat the holiday sacrifices while unshod and unshorn. The point, R. Soloveitchik argues, is that both mourning and holiday joy are internalized emotional states before they are performed rituals, and these emotional states are in total conflict. (The proofs for the internalization of holiday joy, a topic of great interest to R. Soloveitchik, will not occupy us here.) For this reason, then, private mourning can be observed on Sabbath, for it internalizes honor and dignity, not joy, and honor and dignity do not conflict emotionally with mourning.[8]

Rabbi Soloveitchik also correlates this discussion with the fact that a leper observes all the norms derived from the mourning-pattern, even on festivals. (The very imposition upon both the leper and the excommunicate of the norms of mourning offers, of course, an interesting insight into the common qualities of all three situations, and the Rav develops this very point.) Now, this situation is problematic in context, as the festival ought deflect the leper's "mourning" much as it does that of the bereaved. The Rav argues to the contrary that the leper's removal from the community—which the Torah insists upon independent of the rabbinic imposition of mourning-norms— prevents him from entering physically into the festival celebrations and, consequently, from fully participating in the "communal rejoicing" that deflects the "individual's mourning." This is not precisely another example of the interplay of performance and internalization, but it does demonstrate, again, the connection of mourning behavior with broader patterns of action in a context of values.

A further indication of the internalized nature of mourning is the exemption of the high-priest from mourning ritual (an exemption to which only Maimonides does not subscribe). Now, from the fact that he performs the sacrificial Temple ritual even while in the mourning period of *aninut,* the Talmud infers that the high-priest is perennially in the state similar to that of all Jews during festivals. R. Soloveitchik shows that, for Maimonides at least, the high-priest is perennially in the Temple, in some symbolic sense at least. (The Rav's demonstration of this point is instructive from a methodological perspective: since

---

[8] The Rav apparently alternated between the idea that *kavod* (honor) and *oneg* (delight) of Sabbath possessed internalized correlates and the position that they were purely behavioral: see, as well, *And From There You Shall Seek,* n. 19; *Shiurim* I, pp. 63ff.

Maimonides includes both the ban on all priests to tear their priestly clothes while in the Temple and that on the High Priest to tear his at any time in one and the same negative command, it is argued that they are one and the same ban, and the High Priest is simply considered as always being in the Temple. Maimonidean architectonics participates in the search for the essential.) The festival season and the Temple precincts are correlates, for both locate man in the presence of God, and it is this presence, the Rav claims, which rules out mourning. Indeed, he goes further and asserts (through further analysis of the festival rituals) that existential joy is indeed the response to being in God's presence, while mourning is the experience of His absence. The interplay of normative gesture and normative internalization could not be clearer.

Actually, the claim that grief itself possesses normative status ought come as no surprise. A significant component of the mourning process, after all, is *nihum aveilim* [consoling the bereaved]; indeed, the Talmud measures the bounds of mourning itself by the presence or absence of this phenomenon. *Nihum* presumes, clearly, that grief—to which consolation responds—is normatively present.[9]

If we now turn to the process and structure of the mourning ritual itself as the Rav understands them, we shall see that these dovetail with what we have said up to this point, though R. Soloveitchik does not explicitly draw the connections.

The Rav insists that though most mourning gestures are initiated only after burial, the state of mourning itself commences with the death of the mourned, for Maimonides at least. The major proof for this assertion lies in the fact that Maimonides derives the Biblical status of mourning as a whole from the fact that priests are Biblically banned from participating in Temple worship while in *aninut,* the status of the mourning relative before burial. Now, this inference holds only if Maimonides understands *aninut* to be an aspect of mourning. Yet the period of *aninut* begins with death (as does the command that priests render themselves impure, which, we recall, the Rav also takes to be

---

[9] See, e.g., *Mo'ed Katan* 22a; note as well S. Dickman, ed., R. Menahem Me'iri, *Bet ha Behira to Berakhot,* 2nd ed. (Jerusalem 1965), p. 56, top (to *Berakhot* 16b). There are many other topics in classical halakhah that involve the interplay of behavior and internalization, and yet others where this interplay is moot.

an expression of mourning); and so, the Rav argues, mourning itself begins at the moment of death.

Burial, in this perspective, is merely a functional barrier. The bereaved, simply put, is not expected to engage in all the behavioral gestures of mourning while he is occupied with the task of burial: he is either preoccupied or free of all other positive normative obligations. (The Rav must argue, then, that even the negative gestures—not wearing shoes, for example—are not banned activities, *issurim,* but rather components of the positive structure called mourning.) After burial, however, all the obligations that death itself initiates, become operative. Thus, the Rav notes that these gestures are Torah norms after burial only on the day of death, for it is this latter situation that is generative and crucial. Even the psychological effects of burial as a moment of finality and recognition are not converted into halakhic currency (as they are by others); burial is functional and formal. Death itself contains the fullness of meaning that will be engaged by mourning.

The period from death to burial, then—that period for which the halakhah has devised the category, *aninut*—is a situation in which there are no gestures of mourning even though the state of mourning fully exists. In other words, *aninut* renders actual, in "real time," what the Rav describes analytically when he claims that all mourning can be differentiated into performance and grieving internalization. The behavioral aspect cannot exist without an emotional basis (at least insofar as the seven days of mourning are concerned), but internalization is possible without performance—as *aninut* demonstrates. Indeed, the expression *"aninut"* will also be used as a general term to signify the internal aspect of mourning; the *Mishnah* rules that the relatives of executed criminals do not perform the rituals of mourning, but they do grieve (*oninin),* for "grief is only of the heart" (*she-ein aninut ela ba-lev*).

It is true, of course, that *aninut* itself has behavioral content: it limits many forms of contact with the Temple and Temple-associated rituals. Indeed, this is the basic content of *aninut.* It seems, however, that the dividing line between Temple-ritual and internalization is thin or permeable, inasmuch as the Temple concretizes man's standing in the presence of God—a motif that is primarily spiritual. Thus, it is altogether appropriate for the Rav to argue that, despite the general assumption that mourning is only a rabbinic norm after the day of death itself, there is in fact a full seven-day Torah-mourning period, which is marked by the ban on mourners' presenting sacrifices at the Temple. This, I believe, is the correlate to *aninut*. What the Rav seems to be saying is that mourning as an internalized activity and norm is, of course, the basis for the behavioral patterns of the post-burial, first day of mourning, but that its independent phenomenological integrity is disclosed in both preburial *aninut* and post-burial distancing from the Temple.

The Rav returns to the nature of the *aninut* phase of mourning in a brief discussion of the suspension of normative duties during that period. Here, though, he does not see this suspension simply as a reflex of the task of burial that occupies the mourner; indeed, the radical quality of this situation, in which the mourner is not expected (or allowed) to fulfill any positive norm seems to call for more substantive justification. The Rav suggests that this suspension in fact reflects the existential situation of bereaved man facing death in its most intense and uncompromising brutality, a brutality that threatens to deprive the world of all meaning and, specifically, to dehumanize man himself: ". . . why lay claim to singularity and imago dei? . . . why be committed, why carry the human-moral load? . . . Our commitment to God is rooted in the awareness of human dignity and sanctity. Once the perplexed, despairing individual begins to question whether or not such distinctiveness . . . exists, the whole commitment expires. Man who has faith in himself . . . was chosen and burdened with obligations and commandments. Despairing, skeptical man was not elected. How can man pray and address himself to God if he doubts his very humanity . . . ?"[10] Halakhah, in this case, legitimates man's momentary inability to address God, for it recognizes the coherence of the human reaction

---

[10] "*Aninut* and *Avelut*," in *Out of the Whirlwind*, pp. 2f. (It is not easy to find a Talmudic-rabbinic source for this explanation of our norm, though it may be possible: see *Tosafot Berakhot* 17b, *s.v. patur*, which applies, however, only to *keriat shema* and *tefillin*.) In essence, this is a psychologized variation of the argument already offered in *Halakhic Man*, trans. Lawrence Kaplan (Philadelphia, 1983; first published in Hebrew in 1944), p. 31: "Authentic Judaism . . . sees in death a terrifying contradiction to the whole of religious life. . . . 'One whose dead [relative] lies before him is exempt . . . from all the precepts . . . in the Torah.'"

to death. One is obliged to say *"barukh dayyan emet"* and bless God at the moment of death, but one is also unable to observe His commands. While this discussion of *aninut* is quite different than the one presented earlier on, both discussions focus on the internalized aspects of the mourning experience. From a more general methodological perspective, this interplay of halakhic norm and religious/existential reality is an excellent exemplar of Rabbi Soloveitchik's claim that halakhah is the fundamental authenticator and vehicle of the Jewish worldview.

It should be noted that the Rav's assertion that mourning is both behavioral and internalized does not necessarily reflect a modernizing, Protestantizing bent, which would deny the validity or integrity of behavioral norms unaccompanied by internalization. Thus, despite the modern terminology, the halakhic analysis seems to be autonomous. For one thing, the presence of emotional components in mourning is stressed, as the Rav notes, in certain medieval thinkers—the Tosafists and R. Yehiel of Paris, for example; indeed, this internalization is a consistent motif in the latter's commentary to *Mo'ed Katan*.[11] The Rav also makes it clear that just as there are halakhic topics that fuse the behavioral and the internal—mourning and prayer, for example—so are there topics where this would not be true.[12] Going one step further, he argues that certain components of even the mourning process, such as the thirty-day and year-long mourning periods, lack all internalization. Yet the behavioral-internalized model does seem to have an ideal quality, a halakhic-anthropological richness, for R. Soloveitchik. Indeed, it seems that for the Rav, internalization precedes the halakhic behavior discussed and serves as its basis. He does not describe a situation where behavior is expected to create the appropriate internalization.[13]

Let us conclude our summary at this point. Clearly, there is much that we have not done, both in terms of additional substantive matter and in terms of the analytic treatment involved. Nonetheless, and in the light of the limited purpose we set ourselves, I believe we have given

---

[11] Among *aharonim*, see R. Isser Zalman Meltzer, *Even HaEzel* to *H. Avel* 1, 1–2.

[12] See *Al haTeshuva*, p. 40, and n. 7 above.

[13] See Gary A. Anderson, *A Time to Mourn* (Penn State U. Press, 1991), pp. 1–18. The issue goes much deeper than the specific question of mourning-ritual, of course.

a fair summary of the Rav's thought on this topic as well as a fair taste of the method that has produced it.

We have summarized and occasionally interpreted. We have not evaluated or attempted a critique. How, for example, does the Rav read texts? More specifically, how does his "creativity" sit with the textual evidence itself? Moreover, are there different ways of relating to the problems raised? These are not necessarily carping questions; understanding the "roads not taken" contributes constructively in understanding what was done. Nor have we asked whether there are other materials—uncited by the Rav—that support his analysis.

What I think has been made clear, though, is that Rabbi Soloveitchik mounts questions that penetrate to the heart of the topic discussed and molds the myriad particulars of halakhic discussion into a broad, synthetic structure. He deals with detail, of course—no authentic halakhic discussion could ever forego that—but details are not trivia. I recall that the Rav once dismissed a very popular volume of rabbinic studies as "a collection of halakhic eccentricities." The point about the Rav's own work, though, is not merely that he did not produce halakhic eccentricities. It is, rather, that the Rav thought there was no such thing as a halakhic eccentricity, if halakhah is properly understood.

## IV

Stepping back a bit from the dialectic swirl, a number of further comments can be made. First, as to the immediate discussion before us, which has frequently focused on the interplay of behavior and internalization. So far as I know, the Rav does not deal at length with the nature of mourning as an emotional, internalized state. In the halakhic writings, it is clear that mourning is opposed to festival joy, that it is a state of deep sorrow. He does not, however, offer a characterization of this sorrow or describe its dynamics. The aggadic writings offer a somewhat richer picture. The Rav describes mourning as the inability ever to communicate with loved ones, the absolute sense of loss. He also discusses the sadness and guilt engendered by the realization that one can never set things right again, that the opportunity to renew a relationship and make it whole is now out of one's grasp forever. This, he writes, is what *Hazal* meant by saying that one mourns one's parents because one has lost the chance to "Honor thy father and thy mother"; the Talmudic point is broadly experiential and relational, not narrowly normative. All in all, one does not mourn "the other" who has died; rather, one mourns what has died in oneself.[14]

In the discussion we have studied here, however, grief—the internalization of mourning—is treated as a norm, not as a natural emotion. Just as one is obliged to produce the ritual of mourning behavior, so is one obliged to produce its internalized infrastructure. We seem to be dealing, then, with the interplay of two norms—not with the interplay of norm and human nature. Yet this is undeniably an extreme formulation; it is unrealistic to overlook the basic grounding of mourning emotions in human nature (or the culture we know). Rather, Rabbi Soloveitchik posits the interplay of two norms, one of which is fully a normative construct, the other a norm that bases itself—as do other norms—on the foundation of human nature. (This specific issue leads to certain Maimonidean texts, but that is not our concern here.) The two perspectives on *aninut* given above—as the normative state of non-behavioral mourning and as the normative product of man's instinctive reaction to death—might serve as an analogy.

What, in toto, has the Rav given us here (and I refer to the discussion at hand)? I do not think that terminology like "philosophy of halakhah" is very helpful or accurate. In the essays before us, the topic discussed is not "halakhah" per se, but rather specific areas of halakhic practice, and it is these areas that are discussed, not the enterprise of halakhah in its totality. The term "philosophy" is also not adequate, as it suggests a more systematic and all-embracing presentation than the Rav attempts.

So I think it will be useful to start with the claim that the Rav is presenting an interpretation, in the hermeneutic sense of the term, a sense well described by Charles Taylor: "Interpretation, in the sense relevant to hermeneutics, is an attempt to make clear, to make sense of, an object of study. This object must . . . be a text or a text-analogue

---

[14] See, e.g., *On Repentance*, pp. 279–80.

[I shall later revert to the question of whether the Rav, in the essays before us, discusses texts or text-analogues], which in some way is confused, incomplete, cloudy, seemingly contradictory—in some way or other, unclear. The interpretation aims to bring to light *an underlying coherence or sense* [italics GJB]. . . . What are the criteria of judgment in a hermeneutic science? . . . It makes sense of the original text: what is strange, mystifying, puzzling, contradictory is no longer so, is accounted for."[15] Naturally, as Taylor continues, such success presumes some commonly held view as to what "coherence" and "sense" are, some common "language" spoken by participants in the enterprise. This stipulation, Taylor remarks, is but another way of noting the familiar problem of the "hermeneutic circle." I think we can agree that the adjectives assembled by Taylor do, in any case, describe the goals of Rabbi Soloveitchik as he approaches halakhic materials; they certainly describe the state of mind created in his listeners.

Now, what is it that the Rav is making "coherent"? The immediate answer would apparently be: "his texts," which are rescued from their inner contradictions. The "objects of study" are the Talmudic text and the Maimonidean materials. In the process, these texts are not merely freed of their contradictions, but are shown to possess an inner conceptual structure, meaning, and depth. In one sense, this is patently the case: the materials discussed are all quotations from these and other textual sources. Yet I would argue that at least in the essays we have discussed, this answer is not sufficient, that more is at stake. Let us recall that halakhic texts are not philosophical disquisitions, but rather, discussions of normative patterns, that is to say, patterns of behavior. Indeed, they attempt, in large part, to structure behavior. We ought, then, to reformulate our earlier description of what the Rav is attempting. He is not only providing a coherent "text"; rather, he is attempting to "interpret" halakhic ritual behavior, to render this "text-analogue"

---

[15] Charles Taylor, *Philosophy and the Human Sciences* (Cambridge U. Press, 1985), pp. 15–17. There is much sense, to be sure, in Hillary Putnam's objection: "I do not know just what 'coherence' is nor do I know where the criteria of 'coherence' are supposed to come from—do they too only have to 'cohere'? If so anyone can reasonably believe anything, provided he has just the right notion of 'coherence'" (*Realism With a Human Face* [Harvard U. Press, 1990] p. 157). But let us recall that the Rav is not concerned with convincing us of the reasonableness of halakhah, but simply with interpreting it.

coherent and meaningful. And so the Rav's discussion moves within the framework of a language that is "common" to both himself and his listeners in two senses. It is, of course, the common "language" of halakhic intellectual discourse within a given analytic conceptual milieu. But it is also the "language" of behavioral coherence within a given normative pattern. The Rav is engaged, in a sense, in the hermeneutic of halakhic behavior—a hermeneutic that draws upon halakhic concepts, values, and, in our case, psychological and emotional facts.

For an example, let us return to our earlier synopsis of the Rav's discussion of impurity: the priest's impurity for his relatives and the impurity of the priest/Nazirite for the abandoned corpse (*met mitsvah*). We recall that the Rav distinguished between the two, arguing that the former was a substantive act of mourning while the latter was instrumental to the responsibility for burial. We also pointed out that especially as regards the priest's impurity, the Rav was not only concerned with how the priest behaved but with why he behaved in that way, that is to say, with the meaning of his behavior: it was an act of mourning. We realize immediately, now, that the Rav's discussion was not only about texts, but about ritualized experience, the ritualized experience of mourning. The "language" of mourning, then, found new and richer expression through the Rav's hermeneutic of impurity than it had earlier possessed. And, having subsequently explored the Rav's argument for the internalized infrastructure of behavioral mourning, we would now assume that impurity—which implies a violation of sanctity and not merely a levitical state—was also related to that infrastructure, giving us further access to both the behavioral pattern and its internalized base. The claim that R. Soloveitchik provides a hermeneutic of halakhic behavior is even more patent as regards his discussion of the interplay of mourning behavior and the emotions of mourning.

In the studies we have considered, then, the Rav is interested in texts that translate into experience. Perhaps the success of these studies lies in the dual coherence that is achieved. There is, first, the immanent normative coherence: rules and the supporting discussion are integrated with other rules; consistency is achieved; broad over-arching patterns of meaning emerge; straggling trees are shaped into a clearly discernible forest, and phenomena become a cosmos. Each individual detail gains depth, coherence, and conviction; each is rooted in a significant generalization. Second, there is the matter of experiential coherence, for behavior itself is interpreted. The behavior with which these studies deal may be purely ritualistic, constituted as it were by normative rules (as is the case with impurity). Or it may be behavior that, while governed by norms, is expressive at a more universal human level (as is the case with various normative gestures of mourning expressive of grief). In either case, one rises from a reading of these studies with the feeling that the Rav has made halakhic experience more humanly coherent; indeed, that human experience is deepened as it is shaped and molded by the normative performance.

If halakhic concepts and norms do shape and inform the gestures of mourning, if the interpreter of these gestures can successfully turn to this realm of meaning so as to understand the basis of halakhic behavior, it may be useful to descibe Rabbi Soloveitchik's efforts in terms similar to those in which Clifford Geertz describes what he calls "interpretive explanation": "Interpretive explanation . . . trains its attention on what institutions, actions, images, utterances, events, customs, . . . mean to those whose institutions, actions, customs, . . . they are. As a result it issues . . . in constructions like Burkhardt's, Weber's, or Freud's: systematic unpackings of the conceptual world in which condottiere, Calvinists, or paranoids live."[16] The key terms and assumptions sound familiar. One deals with meaning as it is intrinsic to those whose culture is being interpreted. One looks for the "systematic unpacking of the conceptual world" that the participants of the given culture live in their behavior.

Having wandered this far into hermeneutic territory, it is difficult not to push on a bit further, though my comments will be introductory and even telegraphic. Here I will not restrict myself to the specific topic of mourning but will address the broader claims made in *Halakhic Man*. There, as is well known, R. Soloveitchik develops the idea that the halakhic personality perceives reality through the lenses of halakhic categories; the story of Rav Moshe's vision of sunset

---

[16] C. Geertz, *Local Knowledge* (New York, 1983), p. 22.

on *Yom Kippur* (. . . "This sunset differs from ordinary sunsets, for with it, forgiveness is bestowed upon us for our sins") is the famous instantiation of that assertion.[17] It is frequently said that R. Soloveitchik owes this understanding of halakhah as an epistemological tool that enables man to approach and indeed grasp reality, to his Kantian training. Now, this may be true on a biographical level, given the fact that *Ish ha-Halakhah* was published in 1944, and that *Halakhic Mind,* written about the same time, applies similar philosophical concepts to the physical world.

Yet it is difficult, speaking in the 1990s, not to be struck by the congruence of the perspective provided by *Halakhic Man* with certain facets of the work of people like Berger, Geertz, Taylor, Walzer, and others. We may safely disregard the relativistic position of the proponents of "local knowledge" or "communitarianism," which is not relevant to the point I wish to make; indeed, it can even be claimed that their materials and analysis need not necessarily lead to this relativistic position.[18] What we ought pay attention to, I think, is the way norms are taken, in the body of this work, as tools for world-building and world-perceiving. Cultures and peoples, in this view, do not merely regulate their behavior—their interaction with an existing world—through normative patterns. In some sense, rather, reality itself is perceived and structured by the normative pattern, or to quote Geertz again, "They do not just regulate behavior, they construe it."[19] Though this may sound too extreme for Rabbi Soloveitchik's understanding of halakhah, it does capture something of what is going on in *Halakhic Man.*

---

[17] *Halakhic Man,* p. 38; see also pp. 20–24 for other instances. Clearly, though, the halakhic norm is not the exclusive mode by which reality is perceived, as the incident concerning R. Hayyim (p. 36) indicates.

[18] See, for example, the comments of H. Nussbaum, "Non-Relative Virtue: An Aristotelian Approach," in H. Nussbaum, ed., *The Quality of Life* (Oxford U. Press, 1993), 260ff.

[19] *Op. cit.,* p. 215. Note also Geertz' comment about the "imaginative, . . . constructive, . . . interpretive power . . . of culture." (Perhaps Cassirer is a kind of bridge between this hermeneutic school and Kant; the role of Cassirer has been discussed at length by Rosenak, I now note.) The analogy I am suggesting here has already been noted by Kaplan, "Rabbi Joseph B. Soloveitchik's Philosophy of Halakhah," *Jewish Law Annual* 7 (1988), p. 162.

# On Death

My initial reaction to the suggestion that I investigate R. So-loveitchik's approach to death was to devote my discussion to the topic of mourning, namely, the halakhic/normative framework for dealing with death (that of another person, of course). The Rav himself frequently focused attention on mourning, precisely through an examination of its halakhic norms, and I too have dealt with the topic of mourning in the Rav's thought, a fact that would have simplified my task.[1] It became clear to me, however, that I could not avoid a frontal discussion of the issue of death in the Rav's writings. It should be noted that I shall not relate to that class of death that stands out in its moral value—a martyr's death for the sanctification of God's name. The Rav's concern was with death as an existential experience that every individual faces, both in his consciousness and in his life. So while I shall also touch upon mourning, I shall do so only in passing.

Furthermore, a reading of the Rav's most widely known writings—and here the reference is to *Halakhic Man* in particular—is liable to lead us to the conclusion that the issue of death was of no interest to the Rav and that he did not think it of any great significance. Well known are the proclamations that halakhic man does not concern himself with death and that he even abhors being close to it, the description of the Torah authority who became filled with melancholy and despair when he reflected upon death, and the stories of the halakhic giants and family members who never visited cemeteries. Death is the realm where man is powerless to fulfill the Torah's commandments, and therefore it

---

[1] See Yitzhak B. Gottlieb, "*Al Gishato ha-Hilkhatit shel ha-Rav Y. D. Soloveitchik*," pp. 186–97; and "The Norms and Nature of Mourning" in this volume. I thank Prof. David Shatz, with whom I had several "electronic" discussions concerning the matter under discussion, for his comments and references.

has nothing to offer him. Death is measured by halakhic standards and precisely as such it has little standing in the Rav's thought.[2] On the other hand, it seems that "the lady doth protest too much." The Rav's need to declare that halakhic man does not occupy himself with death and the need of halakhic authorities to contend with death, whether through conscious avoidance or through the study of its laws as a way of conquering death and turning it into an objective topos, once again attest to the central place that it enjoys in the Rav's consciousness, if not in his teachings.

Similar to this is the Rav's attitude toward evil in general, which finds expression in his widely read essay, "Hark, My Beloved Knocks" [Kol Dodi Dofek] (but also in other works). The Rav vigorously argues that one should not ask *why* evil exists; the only question to ask is *how* should one deal with it, *what* should be done in relation to it. What should be done, and not why does it happen. This restriction certainly prevents searching after the meaning of death and examining man's existential relationship to it. It also leads us to expect that the topic will be ignored in the Rav's writings.

While the impression is given in *Halakhic Man* that halakhic Judaism deals in practice with the daily improvement of the world in the social and technological realms, this requires some nuancing. So too regarding the statement attributed to R. Hayyim of Brisk that the role of the rabbi in his community is to defend the weak and the destitute an actual description of reality. Perhaps it would be more correct to say that the Rav has other ideas in mind. First, that normative Judaism directs man to all-encompassing cultural and scientific activity and does not demand that he abstain from activity in the mundane world.[3]

And second, that the desired activity is indeed sometimes a halakhic-educational-ritualistic activity. Therefore the appropriate

[2] *Halakhic Man*, pp. 30–37. This work was first published (in Hebrew) in 1944. For a broad discussion of these passages, see D. Schwartz, *Haguto ha-Philosophit shel ha-Rav Soloveitchik*, I (Ramat Gan, 5765), under "death" in the index.

[3] See, however, as regards R. Hayyim in Brisk: Meir Bar-Ilan, *Me-Volozhin ad Yerushalyim* I (Tel Aviv, 1971), p. 235.

question remains: "How should we handle suffering?" "Our inquiry aims at a halakhah of suffering" (127).[4]

But his resolute words in *Halakhic Man* notwithstanding, it is entirely possible that in the rest of his writings and lectures the Rav does not avoid the issue of death in its broad sense or deny the religious importance of the phenomenon. What draws the Rav to this topic is, apparently, its close connection to the issues of suffering and self-sacrifice. Despite the assumption that suffering is evil, and as such one should only learn "how to handle it," the Rav also sees the acceptance of suffering as having an important religious dimension. Suffering frequently leads to death. On the other hand, the Rav is at times exceedingly careful to distinguish between affliction and death and to make sure that the one does not slide into the realm of the other. We too then will have to examine the extent to which the Rav is drawn to the issue of death through his preoccupation with the issue of suffering and to what extent he is careful to distinguish between the two.

We shall, however, open with the laws of mourning, and specifically with the manner in which they function in the Rav's thinking. First of all, it seems that mourning exemplifies two aspects of the Rav's halakhic thinking in general. First, if indeed the Rav repeatedly states that regarding evil one must ask "what one should do," rather than "why," then mourning falls into the category of doing rather than that of understanding or offering an answer. It does not justify God's deed (unless we consider the declaration of "Blessed is the True Judge"). Second, mourning, according to the Rav, consists of both an outer-objective dimension (as he terms it: the "act," or "*ma'aseh*" of the mitsvah) and an inner-subjective dimension (as he terms it: the "fulfillment," or "*kiyyum*" of the mitsvah). These two dimensions find expression and even become integrated in the halakhic regime in our case, for example, when the obligations of mourning conflict with rejoicing on a festival. Thus, mourning joins the ranks of *mitsvot* (including prayer and honoring one's parents) that express the entirety of halakhah in its two dimensions.

---

[4] Page references in parentheses in this chapter refer to Joseph B. Soloveitchik, *Out of the Whirlwind*, eds. David Shatz, Joel B. Wolowelsky, and Reuven Ziegler (Meotzar Harav/ KTAV, Jersey City, 2003).

There is also another aspect to the laws of mourning as the Rav understood them that should be emphasized in light of its religious and conceptual boldness, and also for the light it sheds on the Rav's approach to death. According to halakhah, a person whose dead relative lies before him, that is, a mourner whose deceased relative has not yet been buried, is exempt from all the commandments (i.e., the positive precepts; the mourner is not permitted to murder, or to desecrate the Sabbath). This halakhic fact is already quite bold and surprising. For an entire day, a Jew is granted a blanket allowance not to observe the commandments (and according to one understanding, he is even forbidden to observe them)! The Talmudic rationales are either formalistic or practical. The Rav's approach, on the other hand, is exceedingly fundamental. The observance of *mitsvot*, he argues, is founded on the respect that a person has for himself as an individual standing with dignity before God. Sickening death—also the death of the other over which he must mourn—in contrast, destroys a person's self-respect and proves his nullity. In such a situation, a person is not capable of fulfilling the commandments, nor does he even want to fulfill them. The mourner's exemption from all the commandments is a confirmation of this (temporary) rebellion. This rationale proposed by R. Soloveitchik sheds light both on his understanding of death, to which in the manner of *Halakhic Man* he assigns no spiritual value, and on his understanding of halakhah and its relationship to the inner world of the individual. In our case, halakhah reflects reality and does not fight against it or attempt to reconstruct it.

This reality exposes death in all its ugliness, including its simple, crude ugliness. "The halakhah has never tried to gloss over the sorrowful, ugly spectacle of dying man" (2), and the reference here is not solely to spiritual ugliness. Man is filled with "fright and confusion when confronted with death." Moreover, death destroys the image of God in man in the sense that it removes his spiritual personality from the world and undermines the self-respect of the living. Death disgusts, and the process leading to it humiliates. Just as halakhah is worldly, so too the halakhic man may not ignore worldly phenomenon, and exchange it for some sweet and innocent alternative reality. This motif finds explicit expression in the seventh chapter of *Halakhic Man*, where the Rav distinguishes between "halakhic man" and "*homo religiosus*": the *homo religiosus* longs for a transcendent world, and at the same time sanctifies death as the "threshold to transcendence." Not so the halakhic man, who clings to the earthly as the arena of holiness and denies death any value of sanctity: "A corpse defiles; a grave defiles; a person who has been defiled by a corpse is defiled for seven days and is forbidden to eat any sacred offerings or enter the Temple . . . the priests of God are forbidden to defile themselves with the dead."[5] Judaism "abhors death, organic decay, and dissolution. It bids one to choose life and sanctify it." Therefore, great Jewish scholars, the Rav relates, rarely visited cemeteries or prostrated themselves upon the graves of their ancestors. Despite their faith in life in the World-to-come, they were terrified of death.

## II

Before we enter into the thick of the issue of death in the teachings of Rav Soloveitchik, we should first dwell upon several aspects of the issue that are not unique to the Rav. I refer to what aspects may be called the moral and educational aspects of the topic in the broad sense. What is interesting, and sometimes surprising, is that the Rav adopted these ideas.

Such an understanding appears in an essay appearing in *Out of the Whirlwind,* where the Rav writes that "death . . . is an evil experience if viewed from the perspective of individual existence. However, if seen under the aspect of the total destiny of man as such, the elimination of the old and obsolete or the departure of people who belong mentally to a different age is the greatest of blessings" (126–27). Many have noted that death is the price of renewal and enrichment. Here the Rav adopts this idea not primarily on the biological plane, but on the cultural level. The Rav's acceptance of the idea that by the nature of things certain people reflect the old that must pass from this world, and that their mental attachment to the past demands their replacement by others who are more appropriate for the present, and calling

---

[5] *Halakhic Man*, p. 31.

this natural process "the greatest of blessings," is surprising in its realism, its lack of sentimentality.

The Rav also finds that death bestows a heroic dimension upon life: "Death gives man the opportunity . . . to build even though he knows that he will not live to enjoy the sight of the magnificent edifice in whose construction he is engaged . . . to enrich—not himself, but coming generations. Death teaches man to transcend his physical self and to identify with the timeless covenantal community . . . it enhances his role as a historic being and sensitizes his moral consciousness" (4). Here the Rav makes use of the words of R. Tarfon: "The day is short, the task is great, and the Master is demanding," but he clearly explains them in accordance with his own approach: the day is short—because death prepares an ambush in close proximity; the task is great—and by the nature of things, you cannot complete it; the Master is demanding—that you do what is imposed upon you to do.[6] This is not a Sisyphean endeavor, but there is also no possibility of bringing matters to a successful conclusion.

It is precisely death, argues the Rav, that provides man with this heroic/moral opportunity; were man to live an eternal life, it would be denied him.

This idea appears to be an adaptation of a simpler and more prevalent concept, namely, the notion that man only finds his eternity in the lives of his descendants, only that here the moral dimension fills the vacuum. In general, the Rav's approach emphasizes death as the experience of the individual, thus according with the existentialist school and modernity; the social dimension, which indeed existed in ancient times and in the middle ages, and still exists in traditional societies, is denied and finds no expression. The Rav's account draws from modern experience.[7]

---

[6] *Avot* 2:14. The Rav undoubtedly paid attention to the next *Mishnah*: "You are not called upon to complete the task, yet you are not free to evade it." Most commentators understand the *Mishnah* as referring to Torah study. For the Rav's interpretation, see *Guide of the Perplexed*, III, 10, in relation to the reading in R. Meir's Torah scroll: "And behold, death is good." See also S. Klein-Breslavi, *Perush ha-Rambam le-Sippur Beri'at ha-Olam* (Jerusalem, 5738), pp. 109–13.

[7] Norbert Elias, in *The Loneliness of the Dying* (Blackwell, 1985), argues for the modern context of the loneness and detachedness of death. Here is one of many passages (p. 60): "The special accent taken on in the modern period by the idea that one dies alone matches the accentuation in this period of the feeling that one lives alone. In this respect, too, the image of one's death is

# III

Despite the assertion that "sanctity is rooted in joy," the Rav also stresses the spiritual value of retreat, collapse, submission, and despair.[8] According to the Rav, these are fundamental elements of Jewish spiritual existence. "Majesty and Humility" and "Catharsis" are devoted to the illustration of this motif. The readiness to submit, to waive victory, finds expression in fundamental Biblical gestures—in the conduct of our father Abraham who was ready to sacrifice his beloved son, in Jacob's willingness to set the angel free to go on his way, in Aaron the priest's silence in the face of the death of his two sons in the Tabernacle. But retreat is also required in the daily life of the halakhic man. A favorite example of the Rav's is the bridegroom's withdrawal on his wedding night: "Bride and bridegroom are young, physically strong and passionately in love with each other. Both have patiently waited for this rendezvous to take place. Just one more step and their love would have been fulfilled, a vision realized. Suddenly the bride and groom make a movement of recoil. He, gallantly, like a chivalrous knight, exhibits paradoxical heroism. He creates his own defeat."[9] The Rav continues to argue that the cathartic retreat is required of man not only in the hedonic realm, but in the emotional, religious, and intellectual realms as well. It is irrelevant for our purposes whether the Rav is persuasive in his argument that this motif is indeed Biblical-Rabbinic, or whether perhaps it was created in the Rav's own Bet Midrash, in his rich mental library. What is important is the substance: submission and retreat are

---

closely connected to the image of oneself, of one's own life." Elias also knows (ibid., p. 64) that, "if a person must feel while dying that, though still alive, he or she has scarcely any significance for other people, that person is truly alone." As a sociologist, Elias occupies himself not only with the "idea," but also with the social reality that is either embracing or alienating. For a critique of Heidegger's teachings on death regarding a similar point, see J. Choron, *Death and Western Thought* (New York, 1963), pp. 222–64; and similarly the chapter on death in R. G. Olson, *An Introduction to Existentialism* (New York, 1962), pp. 192–212. Of course, the emphasis on the individual marks the Rav's thought along the entire way and in every context.

[8] Lawrence Kaplan argues that this motif plays a central role in the Rav's thought beginning in the early sixties. See Lawrence Kaplan, "From Cooperation to Conflict: Rabbi Prof. Emanuel Rackman, Rav Joseph B. Soloveitchik, and the Evolution of American Modern Orthodoxy," *Modern Judaism* 30:1 (2010).

[9] Joseph B. Soloveitchik, "Catharsis," *Tradition* 17:2 (Spring, 1978), p. 45. Available at www .traditiononline.org."

central values in the Rav's thought. It would seem that this should also influence his perception of death; it is precisely here that we can locate his attitude toward death that has evaded us until now.

It is tempting to ask: What is the most absolute collapse, the most complete withdrawal, if not the waiver of life in the encounter with death? Here man reaches ultimate submission. It should be noted that R. Naftali Tsvi Yehudah Berlin interpreted R. Akiva's statement, "'With all your soul'—even if he takes away your soul," as referring not to willingness to die a martyr's death for the sanctification of God's name but rather to the love of God at the time of death—every death—in general, at the time that the soul is taken back.[10] Will the perfect man, who is familiar with the ideas of retreat and submission, not realize this love? Does the teaching of submission not lead to this worship? And in the spirit of these words: "If man comprehends the role of a servant of God, then his life is one long service, and death is the conclusion of this hallowed service," but "if the Divine call is ignored, he lives in vain and dies in a very absurd manner" (150).

But there are even more explicit statements: "In death and in suffering one is born to a new true life" (97). Maimonides, according to the Rav, "identifies death with deliverance. To die means to gain freedom from captivity, to join the beloved friend for whom the soul has been yearning all along." These words were stated in a very specific context, the transcendental motif in thematic halakhah. But they must not be disregarded. It is interesting that the Rav admits that he himself was unsuccessful in relieving the real suffering of "the distraught individual who floats aimlessly in all-encompassing blackness," when using the motif of universalism employed by the thematic halakhah—but he says nothing similar with regards to the motif of transcendentalism, despite the comparison that he draws between the two motifs (100). The Rav demands of the individual that he stop viewing himself "in the mirror of immortality . . . When one frees himself from this obsession . . . he learns to take defeat courageously" (132). If the illusion of eternity is the obsession from which man must liberate himself, with what "defeat" are we dealing here if not death? Indeed, the Rav is also capable of speaking of "the

---

[10] *Ha-Amek She'elah* 101:1.

redemption effected by returning my existence to its owner," which may
be understood as pointing to any act in which a person sacrifices his own
desires but may also be read as an allusion to death.

This last sentence appears in the essay, "The Crisis of Human Finitude," where the Rav outlines a way of dealing emotionally with human
finitude. "Judaism . . . wants him to give away something which he has
never received . . . something which he aspires to attain yet which will
always remain outside of his reach. In a word, he must relinquish an
illusion, a dream, a vain hope" (159). What more than anything else
expresses finitude if not death; what is the illusion if not the illusion
of eternity? This essay deals with man's limitations in general, with the
certainty that he will reach his end without exhausting his potential
or fully realizing his strengths, but of course death cannot be excluded
from this generalization. The Rav's sensitivity to finitude finds expression elsewhere as well: "the finitedness of man . . . the absurdity of
living while knowing that one is headed toward the grave. . . . puts an
end to all aspirations, visions, and commitments."[11]

On the other hand, retreat, sacrifice, and failure in the Rav's teachings are almost always found in dialectical movement.[12] Despite the con-
tinuous presence of self-sacrifice and failure in the Rav's thinking, his halakhic teaching—as he himself insists in several places—is an optimistic
teaching; in fact, "better created than not having been created."[13] Even
finitude is a "crisis," and from crisis one recovers; and even the crisis of
death invites heroic action. Almost without exception, man falls solely
to rise again with increased strength. He falls only so that he may know
how to achieve true ascent. On this dialectical plane, there is no room for
final failure, and there is no room to see death as the perfect fall, for death
leaves no room for continuation; and even the fall itself takes place in life.
David Hartman correctly noted that the Rav's use of the motif of falling

---

[11] "The Megillah and Human Destiny" in *Days of Deliverance*, p. 32. This essay has other implications for a discussion of death in the Rav's thought.

[12] See "The Crisis of Human Finitude," p. 176, where the Rav characterizes Job as one who
"lacked the dialectical experience." Until that point, Job "sinned" in that he did not suffer prior
to his encounter with Satan.

[13] See D. Rynhold and M. Harris, "Modernity and Jewish Orthodoxy: Nietzsche and Soloveitchik on Life-Affirmation, Asceticism, and Repentance," *Harvard Theological Review* 101
(2008), pp. 1–32. I wish to thank Prof. David Shatz for referring me to this article.

in Eve's formation from the body of Adam in his sleep, also comes to teach the interpersonal and moral lesson that man is asked to make room for the existence of the other, which translates into the sacrifice of the personal ego.[14] This is also the story of the bride and the bridegroom who sacrifice their happiness on the altar of halakhah: "Sex, if unredeemed, may turn into a brutal, ugly performance . . . Sex, therefore, is in need of redemption . . . What action did Judaism recommend to man in order to achieve this purpose? The movement of withdrawal and defeat."[15] Retreat comes in the midst of life so that the continuation should be more delicate, more human.

This pattern is also found in regard to the experience of nihility, as it were, that encompasses a person when he opens himself to revelation. This experience shows man his nullity as opposed to the fullness of God, but man is not annihilated or destroyed as a result.[16] On the contrary, he will continue to live a life that is permeated with the consciousness of the presence of God. The same is true in each and every realm: "It is obvious that after man has taken defeat at his own hands . . . the pendulum begins to swing in the opposite direction, to the pole of greatness, vastness, conquest, victory and triumph . . . And of course, again, when he finds himself near his destination he retreats . . ."(157f). This dialectical movement finds expression in "A Halakhic Approach to Suffering" (in *Out of the Whirlwind),* "Majesty and Humility," and "Catharsis."

It is precisely his commitment to this dialectic that brings the Rav to warn against inferring an overly optimistic teaching from his words. At the end of his essay, "Majesty and Humility," the Rav adds: "What happens after man makes his movement of recoil and retreats? God may instruct him to resume his march to victory and move onward in conquest and triumph," and this is because "the readiness to accept

---

[14] David Hartman, *Love and Terror in the God Encounter* (Woodstock, 2001), pp. 108–11. See also Rashi's commentary to Genesis 2:19, where he effectively argues that the creation of the woman required of Adam that he surrender his exclusive and Divine standing in the universe.

[15] Joseph B. Soloveitchik, "Majesty and Humility," *Tradition* 17:2 (Spring, 1978), p. 36. Available at www.traditiononline.org.

[16] It seems that the Rav's position on this issue is sort of an expanded commentary on Maimonides' *Hilkhot Yesodei ha-Torah* 2:2, only that the Rav does not deal with man's encounter with creation, but with his encounter with the Creator.

defeat purges the uncontrollable lust for victory."[17] The fall, then, is
an educational and cathartic act; it is not the final destination. But
the Rav is also well aware that the story doesn't always have a happy
ending. Isaac was restored to Abraham, but the Rav sadly admits that,
"Moses was less fortunate. He withdrew; he gazed upon the land from
afar; but his prayers were not answered . . . his total obedience did not
result in victory."[18] The dialectic is so strong that the Rav finds it necessary to restrain it: "Modern man loses a few battles in his struggle with
evil . . . just go into a hospital for incurable diseases and see . . ." Nevertheless, and in face of this known reality, the Rav himself bounces back
and says: "But still modern man says . . . that when one is confronted
by evil, one must face adversity courageously" (104).

## IV

As opposed to what is stated in *Halakhic Man,* the consciousness of
death—especially the consciousness of "my death"—plays an essential
though painful role. Accordingly, immediately following the statement
that "in death and in suffering one is born to a new true life," the Rav
continues by saying that "the pathos, the fear of death, is the mysteri-
ous link between a shadowy experience and true being" (97). And this
apparently is also what he means when he speaks of man's being born
to a new and true life "in death." The reference is not to factual death,
but to death as part of human consciousness. The Rav describes several
experiences that teach man the value of his existence. One experience
is that of disease, and a second experience, as mentioned earlier, is that
of revelation.

The experience of disease is described in autobiographical passages,
where the Rav recounts his ordeals and prayers on the night before his
cancer surgery. That night he had an insight that severed him from the
"illusory immortality" to which man clings, even one who knows intellectually that when his time comes he will die—and the Rav believes
that everyone knows this—but the knowledge itself is mere knowledge,
and doesn't reach the level of experience (131). The fall from "illusory

---

[17] "Majesty and Humility," p. 37.

[18] Ibid., n. 21.

immortality" contributed to a more correct framing of daily experience, its frustrations and disillusions. But more than that, the Rav says
that the inner change that passed over him raised him to a new existential consciousness, one that was more true and authentic (132), and
it stands to reason that this new existential consciousness brought a
change in his daily life. With this insight the Rav is one with the existential school, which demands of man that he internalize the fact of
his own death and not content himself with the "objective" knowledge
that recognizes the universality of death. And indeed, immediately before his account of the night he experienced his own personal transi-
tion, the Rav refers to *The Death of Ivan Illich,* where Tolstoy criticizes
the weakness of objective knowledge regarding death, a story that was
used extensively in existentialist writing beginning with Heidegger.

The second experience that exposes a person to his own nihility
is, surprisingly enough, revelation. It is precisely the individual who
encounters God who recoils to the point of feeling a loss of identity.
"The meeting with nihility . . . takes place when the individual existence is threatened with extinction," as we have just seen. The Rav,
however, also recognizes "the existential bankruptcy of man who has
met with God—with the Being *per se* who both bolsters and negates
other beings, whose existence is all-inclusive . . . who raises man to the
pinnacle of exultation and also lets him sink in the abyss . . . the One
for whom man is questing . . . and from Whom he flees" (123–25).
But what is the logic in this process? The Rav explains: "The apoca-
lyptic trauma of revelation is due to the fact that finite-conditioned
man, confronted suddenly by God, the numinous, all-powerful and
all-negating, becomes aware of the suspension of his own selfhood"
(128). The person who stands before God is exposed to the fullness
that negates his partial and defective existence: "The mere meeting
with God is . . . not only great and blissful but also a shuddering and
horror-filling experience . . . Chancing suddenly upon God, man
becomes aware of his evanescence . . . Infinity swallows up finitude.
What importance can we ascribe to the flickering candle-flame when
it approaches the great all-consuming fire? . . . A bounded being dis-
appears in the eternal boundlessness" (120–21). The conceptual and
psychological background is found in the category of the numinous;

but the Rav is careful to emphasize, in his usual manner, that the process is dialectical. The loss is temporary—there is a second stage, "the moment of ecstasy and rapture which rehabilitates and restores man to heights . . . Meeting God is a glorious and the most blessed event . . . Man becomes transported out of himself and suddenly awakens to new dimensions of reality that were alien to him before" (121). The Rav also speaks in terms of "revelation," which is not the case in Otto's descriptions of the numinous that man encounters. It is also possible to ask whether the Rav was influenced here by midrashic traditions concerning the people of Israel's temporary loss of life when they heard the Ten Commandments: "At every word which went forth from the mouth of the Holy One, blessed be He, the souls of Israel departed . . . But since their souls departed at the first word, how could they receive the second word? He brought down the dew with which He will resurrect the dead and revived them."[19] Or perhaps these traditions were unnecessary for his purposes. (In any event, the Rav also broadens the canvas when he says that suffering and affliction are the bearers of the revelation. From this, by the way, it is clear that the "revelation" about which the Rav speaks is not only the historical experience, but also the personal experience.) God appears in fire, in darkness, in the whirlwind and in gloom; the covenant was made in "the horror of great darkness." According to the Rav, these are not primarily geographical/climactic field conditions, but rather descriptions of the spiritual state of one who is laid open to revelation, to the encounter with God. There is no death here, but there is partial and conditioned nihility, which provides the person with the possibility of lifting himself up anew.[20]

---

[19] *Shabbat* 88b, and elsewhere. A collection of the sources and a discussion about them may be found in Ira Chernus, *Mysticism in Rabbinic Judaism: Studies in the History of Midrash*, pp. 33–73. For a philosophical discussion that is not very far from the Rav's approach, see Emil Fackenheim, *God's Presence in History* (New York, 1970), pp. 15–16.

[20] For a discussion of the philosophical background of these ideas, see Schwartz, *op. cit.* II, pp. 228–90.

# Chapter Sources

A Religious-Zionist Thinker?
Translated by David Strauss from *"HaRav Yosef Dov HaLevi So-loveitchik keHogeh Dati Tsiyoni—HaUmnam?"* in Y. Amir, ed., *Sefer HaYovel le-Eliezer Schweid,* 5765.

Letters on Public Affairs
"Rabbi Joseph B. Soloveitchik's Letters on Public Affairs." *Torah u-Madda Journal* 15 (2008–2009). Translated by Joel Linsider from *Igrot HaRav Y. D. Soloveitchik beInyanei Tsibur,* Yosef Da'at 5770.

Biblical Models
"Biblical Models in the Contemporary Thought of Rabbi Joseph B. Soloveitchik," *Journal of Literature and Theology,* Vol. 8, no. 1, September 1994.

The Jewish People
"On the Jewish People in the Writings of Rabbi Joseph B. Soloveit-chik," *Tradition* 24:3 (1989) 21–43.

"Fate" and "Destiny"
Translated by David Strauss from "Le-Mekorot ha-Musagim 'Gorel' ve-'Yeiud'" in Avi Sagi, ed., *Emuna be-Zemanim Mishtanim,* 5757.

The Covenant of Marriage
Translated by David Strauss from Brit Ha-Nissuin, *Akdamot,* no. 13, April 2003.

The Norms and Nature of Mourning
    "On the Halakhic Thought of Rabbi Joseph B. Soloveitchik: The
Norms and Nature of Mourning," *Tradition* 30:4 (1996).

On Death
    "Death in the Writings of Rabbi Joseph Dov Soloveitchik," *Tradition* 44:1, Spring 2011. Translated by David Strauss from a paper
originally presented in Hebrew at the Van Leer Institute in Jerusalem,
Winter 2010.

# About the Author

GERALD J. (YA'AKOV) BLIDSTEIN, a recipient of the Israel Prize in Jewish Thought and a Fellow of Israel's National Academy of Sciences, is Professor Emeritus in the Department of Jewish Thought at Ben-Gurion University in Beersheva, Israel, and formerly Dean of its Faculty of Humanities and Social Sciences. He received his rabbinic ordination from Yeshiva University's Rabbi Isaac Elchanan Theological Seminary, where he studied under the Rav, Rabbi Joseph B. Soloveitchik.